MW01088042

CARNAL ALCHEMY

CARNAL ALCHEMY

SADO-MAGICAL TECHNIQUES
for Pleasure, Pain,
and Self-Transformation

Stephen E. Flowers, Ph.D., and
Crystal Dawn Flowers

Inner Traditions
Rochester, Vermont • Toronto, Canada

Inner Traditions
One Park Street
Rochester, Vermont 05767
www.InnerTraditions.com

Text stock is SFI certified

Copyright © 1995, 2001, 2013 by Stephen E. Flowers, Ph.D.

Originally published in 1995 by Rûna-Raven Press under the title *Carnal Alchemy: A Sado-Magical Exploration of Pleasure, Pain and Self-Transformation*

All rights reserved. No part of this book may be reproduced or utilized in any form or by any means, electronic or mechanical, including photocopying, recording, or by any information storage and retrieval system, without permission in writing from the publisher.

Library of Congress Cataloging-in-Publication Data

Flowers, Stephen E., 1953–
  Carnal alchemy : sado-magical techniques for pleasure, pain, and self-transformation / Stephen E. Flowers and Crystal Dawn Flowers.
    p. cm.
  Summary: Summary: "BDSM sexuality as a powerful tool for self-transformation and the realization of magical and spiritual aims"—Provided by publisher.
  Includes bibliographical references and index.
  ISBN 978-1-62055-109-7 (pbk.) — ISBN 978-1-62055-154-7 (e-book)
  1. Sadomasochism. 2. Self-actualization (Psychology) 3. Consciousness. I. Flowers, Crystal Dawn. II. Title.
  HQ79.F56 2013
  306.77'5—dc23
                                                                    2013013533

Printed and bound in the United States by Lake Book Manufacturing, Inc. The text stock is SFI certified. The Sustainable Forestry Initiative® program promotes sustainable forest management.

10 9 8 7 6 5 4 3 2 1

Text design and layout by Brian Boynton
This book was typeset in Garamond Premier Pro with Trajan Pro and Gill Sans as display typefaces

Artwork in chapters 1, 2, 3, 5, and conclusion used with permission from Adam Parfrey from the book *Voluptuous Panic: The Erotic World of Weiman Berlin* by Mel Gordon, Feral House Publishing, Fort Townsend, Washington

Permission to quote from *Crafting the Art of Magic* granted by Llewellyn Publications

To send correspondence to the authors of this book, mail a first-class letter to the authors c/o Inner Traditions • Bear & Company, One Park Street, Rochester, VT 05767, and we will forward the communication.

This book is dedicated to the memory of
Mistress J. R.

CONTENTS

CARNAL ALCHEMY

Disclaimer and Warnings

Techniques discussed in this book are intended as theoretical guidelines, not necessarily instructions for actual activity. Do not undertake any of the physical techniques in this book without thorough personal training. Take the same precautions you might before starting a course of rigorous physical fitness that would involve a doctor's approval. Furthermore, the ideas outlined in this book are intended strictly for adult individuals of the age of majority and must be explored in a safe, sane, and consensual environment.

The authors, editors, and publisher of this book accept no responsibility or liability for accident, injury, or mishap that might befall any individual as a result of performing activities depicted herein.

Participation in S-M sexuality inherently involves certain risks—the responsibility for these risks lies entirely with the participant(s). The contents of this book are not intended as a substitute for personal training and consultation: in matters of safety and in the safe and reliable use of equipment we advise in-person guidance.

Notice: Readers should determine the legalities of the possession of certain types of S-M equipment in accordance with the laws of the state in which they reside.

Notice: This book contains nothing that is intended to appeal to prurient interest. It is a book of spiritual philosophy and psychological and sexological education and development.

A Note on Terms Used in This Book

In this initial study of our topic, terms such as "Carnal Alchemy," "Sado-Magic," and "Sado-Shamanism" are used in a fairly indiscriminate fashion to indicate the use of the methods of dominant and submissive sexuality for purposes of self-transformation, sorcery, or other forms of magic. Individual terms are more narrowly defined in the glossary.

PREFACE

TO THE THIRD EDITION

Since the original publication of this book in the early 1990s the world has become much more accepting of S/M sexuality. To a great extent that is what this book was written to facilitate in the early 1990s. Most recently the world has been deluged with the success of the *Fifty Shades of Grey* phenomenon, which has brought the sexuality of dominance and submission to the forefront of popular culture. But with this good has also come some bad—which is what we must come to expect in the world. Five years after the first publication of *Carnal Alchemy* and over fifteen years after the reconstitution of the Order of the Triskelion, the spiritual state of affairs in the world of S/M needs to be reevaluated.

In the 1980s and early 1990s the Order of the Triskelion worked underground and magically to bring S/M sexuality and spirituality more out into the open—and into the mainstream of life. The reason for this is that for many years people were living their lives out in unhappiness. Some could not bring themselves to accept their own desires for S/M experience, while even more were unable to communicate their needs to a sympathetic sexual partner. If this form of sexual expression could be brought out more into the light of day, perhaps it would be easier for everyone to come to terms with his or her own sexual desires and to find a life partner who shared those desires. This was the inner work of the Order of the Triskelion.

Perhaps it was simply an idea whose time had come. A new generation, Generation X, came of age in an era of AIDS. A generation born of the baby boomers who seemed to have used up all the fun and left behind a plague-ridden sexual landscape. A world de Sade could love. In this socio-sexual climate S/M sexuality and "modern primitivism," with its tattooed skin and pierced flesh, found more ready acceptance. Doubtless S/M sexuality worked its beneficial magic in the early 1990s. This magic allowed for continued and even deepened sexual adventure and variation in a relatively safe environment.

But with increased interest and participation in S/M sex by the "masses" something of the old-world flavor of S/M before the 1990s was increasingly lost. In the old days those who dared to explore this forbidden form of sexual expression delved into an inner world of taboos and a social environment fraught with the dangers of rejection and misunderstanding. In the 1990s S/M became the "kink *du jour*."

With the loss of the tension of the taboo, of the forbidden aspect of S/M, the whole phenomenon lost some of its very Sadean character. But this faddish acceptance is doomed to pass, as do all fashion trends. What will be left is a healthier world in which those who have the visceral need for it will find fellow travelers, and those who do not have this need will not feel "uncool" for not participating.

The Order of the Triskelion worked hardest when the S/M scene was virtually unknown. As the cultural phenomenon just described grew, the Order slipped progressively into the shadows. Perhaps it awaits a future reconstitution under another charter. This book continues to be offered to the public that it may provide a set of workable ideas for the expression of operative and spiritual S/M, steeped in the old-world aesthetic, for those who want the best of both worlds.

STEPHEN E. FLOWERS

PREFACE
TO THE FIRST EDITION

This little volume has been written to fill a large gap in the recent literature on sexual magic. Although there has been a long-standing relationship between the infliction of pain, or the suffering of pain and sexual desire and fulfilment, virtually nothing about this aspect of sexuality in the magical field has appeared. This does not mean that such a connection has been non-existent. The historical chapter of this book briefly demonstrates its enduring power in Western culture.

In most recent times the Sadean field of magical study has been the specialty of the Order of the Triskelion, which despite whatever mysterious origins might be ascribed to it, has been exploring the practice of this form of magic for the past several years. (A prospectus of the O∴ T∴ is printed as an appendix to this book.) Several other groups and individuals have also explored various avenues of the powers hidden in the practice we are writing about here. Some of their names and addresses are found in the Resources directory of this volume.

Because of the highly individualistic nature of the symbols and psychological responses involved in working Sado-Magic, most true development can only take place between individuals involved in an intimate relationship. "Groups" of any kind can provide theoretical frameworks, create supportive atmospheres, or act as social environments for certain experiments, but they are not essential to development in Sado-Magic or the Carnal Alchemy. However, a primary relationship seems to be essential. Carnal Alchemy cannot be completely utilized in a solitary environment or in one where casual encounters are the rule.

We must emphasize that techniques discussed in this book are not to be employed without proper training from someone who knows how to employ them. Frater U∴ D∴ , the noted German expert on sexual magic, says of the use of S-M in sex-magic

> . . . [S-M] is a very specialized sexual discipline, which requires some training. In fact the S&M scene worldwide has its own mores, rites, and lingo to which the newcomer has to be thoroughly introduced. Of course, like all things worth learning, the methods of S-M sexuality are often difficult—perhaps impossible for some.[1]

Sadean sexuality is a part of our most ancient heritage, and it will be an increasing part of the future state of liberated humanity. But we must ensure that society as a whole is increasingly educated as to the true nature and ultimate benefits of this type of sexuality, and we must ensure that those practicing this form of sexuality have access to trustworthy information on the subject and that it is treated with the kind of physical, emotional, psychological, and spiritual respect it deserves and requires.

CRYSTAL DAWN AND STEPHEN E. FLOWERS

CARNAL ALCHEMY

SADO-MAGICAL TECHNIQUES
for Pleasure, Pain,
and Self-Transformation

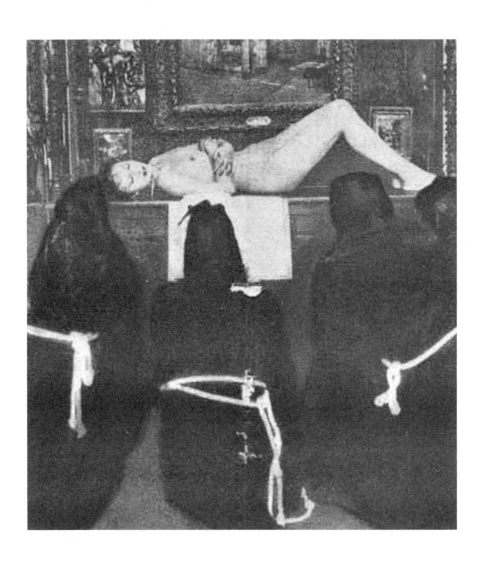

IMPORTANT
SAFETY NOTES

Although this is not intended as a training manual for dominants, because many of the methods touched on in this book can be dangerous to one's health, we are including some thoughts on safety.

- NEVER attempt to tie your partners in any way that will cause them to have to bear their full weight on the bindings. Suspension requires special knowledge and equipment to execute safely.

- NEVER bind your partners anywhere, but especially at the wrists and ankles, with too much tension for too long a time. Pressure at the wrists, for example, can easily cause nerve damage to the hands in a short time.

- NEVER leave your partner bound and unattended.

- NEVER strike a submissive in the kidney area, on the spine, in the face, or in any other potentially dangerous bodily location.

- NEVER break the skin of the submissive with a non-sterile instrument. Needles used for temporary piercings must be sterile and used only once.

- NEVER practice Carnal Alchemy while in a chemically impaired state.

———•———

- ALWAYS provide for some mode of communication with your submissive. You should always have a "safe-word" the submissive can use to tell you that the intensity level has become too great to bear. If the submissive is gagged, provide a hand signal that will serve the same purpose.

- ALWAYS be aware of the presence of bodily fluids and breaks in the skin and take measures to prevent the spread of infections, hepatitis, HIV, and so forth.

- ALWAYS respect any safe-words that have been prearranged.

- ALWAYS be sure that your activities with any partner are safe, sane, and consensual.

1
SEXUAL MAGIC AND CARNAL ALCHEMY

Magic is much more widely practiced than many believe. The famous magician Aleister Crowley once defined "Magick" as "the art and practice of causing changes to occur in conformity with Will."[1] Under this definition many things can be seen for the magic that they are. Too often our senses are dulled to just how magical our existences are. Crowley's definition is, however, too limited in our postmodern age. A more exact definition is needed, especially if we are to work with the powers inherent in the polarity of pleasure and pain.

The true practice of magic depends on the legitimacy of the individual human will. The magician wills something to occur, which under ordinary circumstances would not occur, and thereby demonstrates the reality of his or her own individuality. Magicians make the world dance according to their tunes; religionists seek to find the tune of the world and have it teach them how to dance.

Perhaps the most practical theory of magic presupposes two basic "universes," as human beings usually experience things. One is the subjective universe, which is the interior realm of consciousness—where we find the human will. The other is the objective universe, which is the exterior world with all its laws and forces.

There are two ways of working magic. First the magician can make strategic changes in the objective universe through ordinary physical media to communicate some message to other subjective universes (individual wills) outside their own. These means and the message they carry in turn cause a change to occur in the subjective universes receiving the message. In fact this is a form of communication through "normal channels" (speech, sight, and so on) in which there are also hidden factors working on an unconscious level. Recipients of this will then respond accordingly—depending on how skillfully the communication is done. This sort of magic is practiced in advertising, politics, sexual seduction, and all sorts of other forms of interpersonal communication where one person is trying to influence another to do his or her will. What makes this form of communication magic is that the laws by which this communication works are not open and ordinary, but rather hidden and extraordinary. One person does not simply tell another: "Buy this soap," he uses hidden symbolism (such as sexual fetishes, appeals to ego, and so forth), which are associated with the soap he is trying to sell, only by contact. The buyer then unconsciously associates the two ideas (for example sexual pleasure and this soap) and finds himself buying it the next time he is at the store—but he doesn't know why . . . This type of magic works from the subjective universe of the magician upon the objective universe, changes in which are symbolically responded to by the other subjective universes (human minds) in the area. This process is often known as "lesser magic."

The other kind of magic works more mysteriously. Magicians may make deep internal changes in their own subjective universes, which, in turn, will cause changes to occur directly in the greater objective universe. Such alterations are dependent upon the power and precision of the change or impression made in the subjective universe—or "imagination"—of the magician. These changes will inevitably have their repercussions in the universe as a whole—causing analogous changes to occur there. This is magic as we usually think of it. The magician makes a change in his or her internal universe, and a corresponding change occurs in the outside world—with no logical or objective connection between the two events. This technique is also useful in making permanent changes in the mind or psyche of the magician—which is not as easy as it would at first appear to be. This type of magic symbolically works from the subjective universe of the magician, changes in which eventually surface as objective changes. In this type of magic, symbols are transformed into events or states of being.

How is this done? Magicians stimulate a certain form of consciousness in themselves, then perform certain symbolic acts—utter a set of words accompanied by certain gestures. The results of these acts are then felt at some remote time and place. This process is known as "greater magic."

Most of the Sado-Magic we talk about in this book is of the greater magical variety. The use of sex (and certainly the symbolism of S-M sexuality) is quite common in lesser magic, and it can and should be used in conjunction with greater magical aims. The use of aesthetics, of employing symbolism to appeal to a sense of sexuality, beauty, and awesome power, is a key to triggering states of consciousness in which the magician can effectively express his or her will.

SEXUAL MAGIC

Who can deny the supernatural power of sex? Whether we see it as a conduit for the regeneration of life itself, or as a way to commune with the spirit and soul of another, or as a method for gaining power, over another, the whole subject sparkles with the aura of magic. Sexuality is the most abundant basic power source available to most human beings, and so harnessing it holds out the greatest promise for an abundance of magical power. There is so much free-floating sexual energy and symbolism in our society that it is used for all manner of things not strictly connected with sex. Again advertising examples spring to mind. How many cars, beers, and countless other products are sold on the basis of "sex appeal" despite the fact that the product itself has nothing to do with sex in any logical way? People are also sold a variety of things—cosmetics, diet products, exercise machines—all on the basis that if they don't use them they won't be attractive to potential sexual partners.

But how can this power be harnessed for magical purposes? This subject is often confounded with morality. There is nothing immoral or bad about sexual energies per se, although many religious teachings try to tell us there is. Certain "magical" or "religious" traditions regarding sexual energy or symbolism are designed to sublimate or transmute sexual energy or symbolism into something other than sexual. Sado-Magic tends, on the other hand, to view sexuality as something that is in and of itself "sacred," "holy," or just plain powerful. Therefore, the way to increase or give rise to sexual energy is simply to generate it in ways the individual finds most pleasurable and appealing.

From a practical point of view the main thing about sex-magic is that it works on the basis of sexual energy or arousal. The higher the level of arousal or excitement, the more sexual energy the magician will have to work with.

Every object outside the inner world of the magician, each of which can be sensed by the working magician, is a potential magical tool. In more ordinary forms of traditional magic these can be things such as the sight of the wand, the feel of a dagger, the smell of incense, the sound of a gong, or the taste of wine. If these sensory objects can be symbolically so powerful, then how much more powerfully can the ultimate sensory experiences of sexual pleasure and pain be turned into magical tools?

These sensory objects have two levels of meaning. The first is purely physical or physiological. The buildup and release of energy, in sexual orgasm, for example, is a powerful and magically useful phenomenon. But on another more subtle level this sensation is interpreted symbolically by the psyche—and is thought of as a magical substance as malleable as the ink in the formation of magical sigills.

To work sexual magic most effectively magicians need to learn about themselves sexually. They need to find out what really excites and arouses them. Magicians must learn to ignore and discount social constraints or "peer pressure" when it comes to sexuality. Many people only permit themselves to find sexually exciting those things that have been approved by society, when, in fact, what they would find exciting are things that society would condemn them for. This ranges from the gender of their sexual objects to their sizes, shapes, and so on. How many men pursue the "Miss Suzy Sunshine" type because other men think she is the ideal? And how many women act out the role of "Miss Suzy Sunshine" when they really want to be a "Morticia Addams"? Or how many women, for similar motives, will only date the "Jock," or "businessman-in-suit-and-tie" type, when their hearts might prefer the "Rebel" or "Artist"?

One aspect of traditional sexual magic, such as that found in Indian tantrism, that is often overlooked is the power of the forbidden. Very often instructions for sexual rites tell the participants to eat certain foods, drink certain things, or engage in certain practices in preparation for the actual sexual component of the rite. Almost always these actions are ones that are held to be taboo or forbidden by their society in general. Taboo things contain power. In our society today no type of sexuality is more forbidden than Sado-Masochism. It, therefore, holds out the possibility of being a great reservoir of power. But the Sadean magician should go beyond what society holds to be taboo and explore those taboo areas in his or her own soul as well. Breaking the taboos of society is one thing, but in breaking internal taboos great storehouses of magical power are to be found.

The potential Sado-Magician must know his or her sexual landscape, as it were, and that sexual landscape must include Sadean images and experiences. Make a "sexual inventory" of your fantasies and desires. Then work on expanding and extending them—always remaining "true to thine own self" in what you desire.

Part of what the Order of the Triskelion calls "the Triskelion Process" involves the exploration and expansion of the fantasy life. Many who are now interested in Sadean sexuality have had Sado-Masochistic fantasies since childhood—long before they knew what "vanilla sex" (conventional) was all about. Such people seem to have been "born to it." These explorers are encouraged to return to the childlike spirit of fantasy to discover hidden or forgotten aspects of such a fantasy life. But there are also those who have realized the Sadean interests later in life. Such "late bloomers" probably had repressive childhoods in which they felt they had no internal permission to indulge in such fantasies— which they knew on some level to be forbidden. Some people can benefit from the existing fantasies of others, usually in the form of literature, to stimulate the faculty to fantasize. How many of us were stimulated in this way by reading *Story of O*? Everyone can expand his or her fantasy life by experiencing the stories and myths of others.

The potential sexual magician, whether Sadean or not, should also experiment widely with sexual responses and various ways of producing orgasms. This is usually best done autoerotically. See how long you can stimulate yourself without orgasm. See how many orgasms you can experience in a set period of time. Also refrain from having orgasms for a period of days—observe your response.

The Sado-Magician will also want to experiment autoerotically with various pain techniques. The chapter on "Working Techniques" provides many ideas for those who need some suggestions. Anything you would do to another you should, if possible, experience yourself first—either at the hands of another or at your own hands. In any event, try producing certain levels of pain and gauge your response to it. Learn how you deal with it. Then experiment juxtaposing the production of pain with that of sexual pleasure. Observe the interplay between them.

HISTORY OF SEXUAL MAGIC

Before going on to the next stage of practical work it will be useful for many readers to become familiar with the idea of sexual magic, or sexual mysticism. We do not have the space for an exhaustive treatment of this theme. For this we recommend books in the general bibliography. But what is important to realize at this point is that sexual magic is an ancient and widespread idea with deep roots and a profound meaning—and is not merely a hyperbolic formula for "really good sex" . . .

Perhaps the first thing that comes to mind when one hears the term *sex-magic* is "tantrism." Tantrism is found in both Hindu and Buddhist religious traditions—and both have some connections to Chinese Taoist alchemy in some respects. The often happy amalgamation of sexuality and religion found in certain sects of the East is perhaps shocking to Christian sensibilities—

but would, of course, seem as natural to our own pagan ancestors as it does to present-day post-Christian heathens.

In Hinduism the erotic component of spirituality is perhaps best known through the famous sexual sexo-magical scripture the *Kamasutra* of the sage Vatsyayana, written almost two thousand years ago. A thousand years after the *Kamasutra* the less well-known *Ananga Ranga* of Kalyana Malla was written. These works contain not only advice and instructions on how to practice the sophisticated arts of love but also magical recipes such as

> *The man who, after enjoying his wife, catches some of his own Kama-salila (seminal fluid) in his left hand, and applies it to her left foot, will find her entirely submissive to his will.*
>
> ANANGA RANGA, CHAPTER VII

> *The woman who, before engaging in sexual intercourse, will touch the linga (penis) of her husband with her left foot, and will make a practice of this, will undoubtedly subdue him, and make him her slave for life.*
>
> ANANGA RANGA, CHAPTER VII

Tantrism is essentiality a secret initiatory tradition focused on the worship of the Goddess. For the tantrics this Goddess is understood as the Shakti—or Power—that underlies and runs through everything. Conversely this Power is held or wielded by the God—or Shiva (the Lord). The traditional magic spells just given from the *Ananga Ranga* only fully make sense when one understands the *shakti* inherent in the seminal fluid, the penis, the (left) foot, and so forth.

The Goddess is present in the human body in the form of the Serpent Power (*kundalini*), which lies dormant and coiled at the base of the spine until one learns the secrets of raising it along the spinal column and out the top of the head to attain union either with one's own divinity (*jivatman*) or the absolute (*Atman*).

Tantrism cannot be simply reduced to its sexual practices, but such practices and forms of worship are essential to it—although they are often actualized only symbolically. One of the most important types of worship in tantrism is the *Panchamakara*—or "Five-Ms." These stand for the Sanskrit words *mansa* (meat), *matsya* (fish), *madya* (alcoholic drink), *mudra* (grain), and *maithuna* (sexual intercourse). Each of these is thought in some way to be taboo in orthodox Hinduism—and therefore consciousness must be exercised in order to transmute these patently profane indulgences into sacred acts. After the first four Ms are consumed in a ritual carried out by a male and a female practitioner, they move on to the sexual component of the rite as described by Francis King in *Sexuality, Magic and Perversion*.

> The ritual sexual intercourse begins with the male practitioner drawing a triangular diagram—symbolic of the Goddess and the Serpent Power which is her aspect in the human body—upon his couch. For some time the practitioner worships the Goddess, mentally projecting her image into the triangle he has drawn, and then he calls his female partner. After various ritual purifications lays her upon the couch and then, visualizing himself as the god Shiva and the woman as the wife of Shiva, "offers the father face to the mother face"—i.e., copu-

lates, all the time repeating various traditional mantras . . . and mentally concentrating upon the idea of using the senses as a means of sacrificing to the Goddess.[2]

Clearly, ideas and practices similar to those found in tantrism were in one way or another widespread in the ancient world. The ancient Mesopotamians and Egyptians, as well as the Greeks and Romans and other Western Indo-European peoples had analogous beliefs about the powers of sex—but few if any were ever so explicitly outlined as were those of the tantrics. The tantrics had the added advantage of their tradition surviving and evolving until the present day, whereas in the West the advent of Christianity created an atmosphere hostile to the sacred aspects of sexuality.

In early modern times, however, more direct cultural contact between Europe and the East made it possible for Europeans to become acquainted with the sexual mysticism of Asia and the Middle East. Partially under the influence of this contact there was also a gradual revival of occultism and magic in European culture. This revival may be dated from as early as the beginning of the eighteenth century with the appearance of the Rosicrucians in Germany. One of the principal texts of this society was *The Chymical Wedding of Christian Rosencreutz* (1616), which placed alchemical teachings in a modestly erotic context. But the groundswell of sexual occultism in the West would only come after contact with the Eastern teachings had been established.

One of the first texts produced was that of Edward Sellon: *Annotations Upon the Sacred Writings of the Hindus* (1865). In the middle of the nineteenth century sexual mysticism was the specialized field of secret orders and associations such as the Hermetic Brotherhood of Luxor in Europe and the Brotherhood of Eulis in the United States. While in Germany sexual enlightenment and intellectual speculation on the powers of sex were reaching unprecedented levels of sophistication: in the late nineteenth century Max Ferdinand Sebaldt von Werth was producing volumes of material dedicated to sexual religion and sexual magic, while pioneering physicians such as Sigmund Freud were on the verge of publishing their theories of sexual repression as the root of individual and social ills. In this milieu of sexual reform and nudism there emerged a secret order called the "Ordo Templi Orientis" (O.T.O.). This group may have begun as early as 1895, but its first documented appearance was in 1904. The O.T.O. was founded by a wealthy German metallurgist, Karl Kellner. He, like Christian Rosencreutz before him, was supposed to have traveled to the East and learned the arts and practices of mysticism. That the secret of the O.T.O. was essentially a sexual one was revealed in print for the first time in the 1912 edition of the order's journal the *Oriflamme*. There we read:

> Our order possesses the KEY which opens up all Masonic and Hermetic secrets, namely the teaching of sexual magic, and this teaching explains, without exception, all the secrets of Freemasonry and all systems of religion.

The O.T.O. would be reformed by an English magician, Aleister Crowley, in the years to come—but more about him later.

In essence, the O.T.O. was styled along pseudo-Masonic lines with secrets revealed to members only after they had reached certain stages of initiation. The O.T.O. originally had ten degrees, and it was only in the eighth of these that the secret of sexual magic was revealed. In the eighth degree the initiate was instructed in the practice of masturbatory sexual magic and thus learned how to manage and channel his or her own sexual energies. In the ninth degree various forms of sexual intercourse were introduced. A major offshoot of the O.T.O. is another German order: Fraternitas Saturni—the Brotherhood of Saturn. This was founded by Gregor A. Gregorius in 1926. The documents relating to this order reveal a vast sexual ideology, which is reviewed in our book, *Fraternitas Saturni,** on the subject.

Throughout the latter part of the twentieth century sexual magic and mysticism had virtually become mainstream with articles on tantric sex in women's magazines hawked on supermarket racks. However, the essential nature of sexual magic as something secret—and at least to some extent forbidden— remains. The secret lies in the fact that sexual magic is not something that can be known from books, it must be experienced and only then can it be understood. Sexual magic is a form of physical knowledge. Therefore, any knowledge you gain must be made physical or carnal in order for it to be impressed on your soul and spirit.

PRAGMATIC SEXUAL MAGIC

Despite all the cultural specific systems of magic and religion mentioned in the previous section, the basic precept of Carnal

---

*This book was known previously as *Fire and Ice* and was published by Llewellen in 1990.

Alchemy remains essentially pragmatic. That is, it is based not on culturally specific symbol systems, but on the strength of the sexual responses to the symbols.

Once your preliminary and exploratory sexual experiments have been done, proceed on to attempt an act of sexual magic. This may or may not contain elements of Sado-Magic. An act of sexual magic will generally have four parts: 1) preparation, 2) intensification, 3) release, and 4) breaking. The important thing is to maintain the pragmatic edge. Do not fall into the trap of using unnecessary symbols or culturally specific accoutrements, which may detract from the pure individualized raising of sexual energy.

1) **Preparation:** Always have a definite magical goal in mind before doing any experiment. Take care of all preparations for the Working: clarify the aim and make it unambiguous, make ready all symbols, and fix the procedure you are to follow in your mind. It is useful to have some set way of beginning magical Work. This ritual can be invented by you. It could be as simple as putting on a certain piece of jewelry or speaking a certain set of words, or as complex as a whole ceremony. The important thing is to set time and space apart from the routine world. By doing so you create a "space" where magic can be made to happen. Once ritual space/time has been entered the Working of sex-magic itself can begin.

2) **Intensification:** Pragmatic magicians use whatever means are at their disposal to intensify and build sexual excitement and energy. The most important thing at this point is the buildup of sexual energy itself. Allow the magical focus of the Working to hover in your mind, and be ready to implement it at just the right moment magically. Let your consciousness oscillate between

the erotic focus and the magical focus during this phase. Some schools of thought have it that you should concentrate on your magical focus throughout, while others maintain that it should be brought to bear only at the moment of orgasm.

3) **Release:** After you have built up this energy to the level you desire, "release" it toward its magical aim to do its Work. This may be accomplished with the help of the orgasm or you may sublimate or "swallow" the orgasm. This is done by concentrating on the aim, visualizing its completion while holding the sexual energy at its peak level, then allowing it to dissipate. In either case, a sense of satisfaction or completion is the sign of a successful "release." The symbolic preparations you made for the Working ensure as much as possible that the released energies find their willed target. The actual release is a highly concentrated event of intense power. It is your Work as a magician to have a concentrated aim attached to this event.

4) **Break:** Immediately after the release of "energy" make a psychological break with the conscious magical aim of the Working. If you remain attached to the aim at this point this will perhaps keep the subtle, even unconscious, parts of the process from working on their own as they can. To aid in this you may allow the erotic atmosphere and feelings to rise up full force again as a pleasurable diversion. The formal part of the ritual is now ended, and this formal break is to be consciously recognized by a gesture or other symbolic act.

Experiment with small things at first. Perhaps use these techniques to make subjective changes in yourself to overcome internal blockages or inhibitions. Then move on to more objective changes.

There are many different theoretical models of sexual magic. No one is correct or incorrect. All have something to be said for them. But no one theory or practice can explain everything. Sexual magic is the most subjective form of magic known, because it necessitates sexual responses in the magician, and because these responses are in and of themselves subjective and individualistic. Experimentation is the key to success.

2

SADO-MAGIC IN HISTORY

Throughout history magicians, shamans, and fakirs of all sorts have made use of physical stimulation (or even the deprivation of stimulation) as a key to unlocking inner states of consciousness or to activating faculties that allow their will to influence events in their environments. This stimulation is often interpreted as pleasure, but just as often pain is used.

Everyone is familiar by now with the American Indian initiatory ritual ordeals such as those made popular in the film *A Man Called Horse.* Warriors of the Mandan Sioux tribe were put through an ordeal of pain, which involved their being lifted off the ground suspended by piercings in their pectoral muscles. They would hang there until they received their vision. The Oglala Sioux have the "Sun Dance," which involves similar, if less common rituals.

The priests of the Norse God Odin undergo torturous ordeals in imitation of their God, who is said to have hung for nine nights on the cosmic tree to gain insight into the runes, the secrets of the universe.

In fact, the use of floggings of various kinds as a rite of passage—from boyhood into manhood, or into a secret initiatory religion, such as Mithraism—is widely known among traditional peoples from Africa to the Pacific and to the northern climes of Europe.

The Lacedaemonians, or Spartans, held a Feast of Flagellations before the altar of the Goddess Artemis/Diana. There young boys were severely beaten before the gathered people. The young men were to bear these floggings cheerfully so as to not disgrace their families by showing any fear or pain. In later times these floggings provided a spectacle for the entertainment of the masses. In this and similar rites flogging seems to have taken the place of certain kinds of sacrifice.

It should also be noted that flogging has been a prescribed treatment for various sorts of sicknesses and disorders—both physical and mental—since ancient times. Ancient Greek and Roman medical manuals suggest it as a treatment for things ranging from "lunacy" to a variety of physical maladies. As late as the nineteenth century various medical theorists were defending the medical value of this treatment.

As far as pleasure is concerned, it, too, has been used for transcendental and magical purposes. You only have to think of the whole Indian system of tantrism or the use of sexual energies in various forms of oriental alchemy to realize how much sexual pleasure has played a fascinating role in the development of spiritual or magical powers.

But what if these two methods of accessing personal power were combined? Imagine what forces and what states of mind could be generated by bringing together the techniques of pain and pleasure! That is precisely what Sado-Magic does. Although this may be a novel approach to magic, especially in the pragmatic form that is being presented here, it is by no means a new idea, especially when we look at the history of Western culture.

The most current ideas about the practice of Sado-Magic have been drawn from many sources. From the ancient traditions of various peoples and sects, as well as from modern pioneers in these methods, each has something to teach us.

ANCIENT WAYS IN THE WEST

The ancient Europeans always seem to have been especially fond of this kind of stimulation. This is a trait they share with the Japanese in the Far East. In the most ancient of times their orgiastic Rites of Spring very often involved flagellation in conjunction with sexual activity.

Many of the old sacred "pleasure/pain games" have been preserved in toned-down folk customs—such as the English "Binding Day," or "Hocktide." This "Hocktide" took place over the Monday and Tuesday in the week following the second Tuesday after Easter. On one of these days young girls were tied up and hidden in the woods, later to be hunted by the boys. They were supposed to be provided with a coin with which they could buy their liberation—but if no coin was to be found the boy could "have his way." On the other day of Hocktide, the roles were reversed.

Flagellation with birch branches was always a part of the Rites of Spring in northern climes. The power of the feminine birch was thought to be able to drive out weaknesses and entities that might sap the strength or vitality of the youth. In Christian times the belief was altered so that the power of the birch was thought to be able to "drive out devils." This is why it was used in judicial punishments in early modern times. Judicial birchings were still being conducted as late as the 1970s on the culturally conservative Isle of Man in Britain. (There have been some on that island who would like to see these reinstituted.) Again the folklore of flagellation is probably best preserved in England—and it is no wonder sexual flagellation has been referred to for centuries (even by the amorous French) as *le vice anglais*—the English vice.

But such uses of flagellation in conjunction with sexual rites were by no means limited to the northern latitudes in Europe. Even the most archaic practices of the Roman Lupercalia also had sacred, if Sado-Masochistic, overtones. This festival was celebrated on or about the fourteenth of February ("the month of purification"). This was to become St. Valentine's Day in the Christian calendar. Its original function was to "purify" nature. To the ancients this had a different meaning from what it was to get in Christian times. To the pagans this "purification" was a banishing of weakness and illness and a strengthening of the forces of nature—including human flesh—to make them vital and powerful. A central custom of the old Roman Lupercalia involved the young men of the town dressing in wolf skins and arming themselves with whips made of thongs of wolf hide. They would then roam the streets hunting for young girls who, when caught, had to bare their flesh to be whipped.

Many of these customs had already died out or lost their immediate erotic content in ancient times. The Roman poet Ovid reported on the whipping activities of the Lupercalia, explaining that they are not the way they used to be, since now the ladies merely present the palms of their hands to be lightly spanked by the wolf-hide whips. But his tone seems to indicate that there was still something he regarded as "uncivilized" about these customs.

In the Roman city of Pompeii, buried and thus perfectly preserved by an eruption of Mt. Vesuvius in 79 CE, there was discovered a "Villa of the Mysteries." On the walls of this building, scenes of various stages of initiation are depicted. One of these shows a young woman lying over the lap of an older one. The younger one is being thrashed across her back with a rod wielded by a wingéd feminine divinity. Several of the Mystery cults required ritual flagellation as an act of purification before the *mystes* could engage in certain activities. These included the Mysteries of Mithras (which have their ultimate origins in Iran).

In the eastern realm there are further hints at the use of flagellation for magical or spiritual ends. From the Vedas, the oldest sacred scriptures of India, we read of the "honey-whip" (Sanskrit *madhukasha*) in the *Atharva Veda* (IX:1) and in the *Rig Veda* (I:157). In both instances the "honey-whip" is mentioned in connection with the equine Ashvins—twin gods of health and youth. The formula of the "honey-whip" forms a powerful symbol of the nature of the use of flagellation in spiritual pursuits. The sweetness of honey, with its association with deep wisdom, is connected with an instrument of pain. This is also reflected in the liturgy of the Zoroastrians of Iran. There we read in the Yashts that thirty strokes of a whip, called the *Sraoshô-Karana,* were applied before conducting a sacrificial feast. Sraosha is the *yazata,* or God, of Obedience and the Guardian of Prayer in Zoroastrianism. This whip is thought to have an ablutionary effect and to liberate the sufferer from all sin.

Besides these sacred contexts, there also seem to be quite a few depictions in Greek art of what seem to be purely recreational spankings and floggings. But even these may have originally had some holy purpose, although they may not be apparent to most people today. But *we* understand.

As late as the early twentieth century in Russia the ecstatic cult known as the *Khlysti* ("whippers")—of which Rasputin is reputed to have been an initiate—performed rites, which involved prolonged flagellation, ending in an orgy. Although this was done in an ostensibly Christian framework, it was hardly orthodox, and most certainly was a survival of the most ancient rites performed by the ancestors of the participants.

Sexuality in all its forms, and most especially in this form, was suppressed (or sublimated) by the teachings of the medieval church, or pathologized by nineteenth-century "professors." During the twentieth century in European culture, however, the sacred power of sexuality was being rediscovered. The apparently "new" interest in Sado-Masochistic sexuality was really just a renewal of something very ancient in our culture.

In modern times the renewal of the sexual aspects of what came to be called B/D or S/M began as a recreational activity in the form of late eighteenth- and early nineteenth-century "whipping clubs," or "flagellation clubs." The existence of these can be traced from contemporary literature, such as *Fashionable Lectures* and *The Merry Order of St. Bridget* (1857). These "clubs" were gatherings where members of both sexes could meet to carry out sexually oriented and highly ritualized experiments in flagellation. At the same time specialized brothels were being instituted in London, Paris, and Berlin. These brothels, or "message parlours," provided their customers with experiences in every form of bondage, discipline, and flagellation imaginable. One of the most famous and successful of the madams in this field was Theresa Berkley, who even invented her own bondage device (the Berkley Horse). She died in 1836, wealthy from her earnings from her specialized services.

THE JAPANESE TRADITION
KINBAKU-BI

It has been noticed that besides Europe the only other cultural sphere that seems to have embraced Sado-Masochism as a distinct sexual aesthetic is Japan. There are several unique aspects to the Japanese tradition, which we will highlight here. However, it is also important to be aware of the degree to which early twentieth-century European images of Sado-Masochism penetrated Japanese culture at that time.

The predominance of visual aesthetics in Japanese culture is obvious. From Zen gardens to *ikibana*, "flower arrangement," the trend is clear. One of the earliest documented manifestations of a Sado-Masochistic dimension in an artistic context is the art of Ito Seiyu (1882–1961). He was a painter, woodblock artist, photographer, and writer. His work, often based on folktales or ancient manuals, acted as a bridge between old and new Japan. His aesthetic aim is said to have been the depiction of "Beauty in Suffering." He captured the real drama of the edge between pleasure and pain in the fleshly experience of what he was depicting. Seiyu pioneered what became a significant tradition in Japanese (and eventually Euro-American) art, with artists such as Minomura Kou (Toshiyuki Suma).

The depiction of Sado-Masochism has also extended to both literature and film in contemporary Japan. The maiden-in-distress theme is a common one in folktales and in *Kabuki* theater. Artists such as the famous Oniroku Dan (1931–2011) splashed the vision across the twentieth and twenty-first centuries. The world of *anime* and more precisely *hentai*—which explicitly shows scenes of torture and unusual sexuality—are replete with images of Sado-Masochism. This is especially true of the Japanese *manga*, or illustrated novels. Since, at present, Japanese censors ban the depiction of pubic hair or penetration in film or video productions, scenes often have to appear as either live action or animation.

In the early twentieth century as Japan and Europe (especially Germany) grew closer culturally and militarily, there developed a school of art and literature called *ero guro* (*nansensu*), "erotic grotesque (nonsense)" in the 1920s and 1930s. This stemmed from decadent European circles, such as Weimar Berlin. It was suppressed during World War II, but it returned to influence post-war Japanese culture with themes of bondage, torture, and erotic crucifixion.

The most dominant contemporary figure in the Japanese world of Sado-Masochism was Oniroku Dan. He was a writer of over two hundred S&M novels and wrote screenplays for dozens of films between 1974 and 1988. He had a definite and intrinsically Japanese philosophy of Sado-Masochism, which centered on a male fantasy, based on love and viewing a beauty suffering from a sense of shame.

The most conspicuous aspect of Japanese Sado-Masochism is a particular style of rope bondage most popularly called *shibari* in Europe and *kinbaku* in Japan. Shibari is a term derived from the Japanese art of wrapping beautiful packages with twine, whereas kinbaku, "tight binding," harkens back to the martial and judicial roots of Japanese rope bondage. In ancient times prisoners were both detained and tortured using similar bondage techniques, which could either result in comfortable immobility or excruciating pain.

To a great extent kinbaku is an aesthetic exercise or ceremony on the part of the *kinbakushi*, or expert in kinbaku—he ties his object beautifully and observes her beauty as she endures suffering and shame and receives pleasure and humiliation. There is a spiritual dimension to this aesthetic practice. Just as with *ikebana,* "flower arrangement" or *kado,* "way of flowers," where the *samurai* would learn in a meditative way to appreciate beauty and to identify with it and to relax the body, mind, and soul, so, too, does the aesthetically and spiritually aware kinbakushi approach his art. The active partner in the process contemplates the beauty of the sights, sounds, smells, tactile sensations, and even the tastes involved, coupled with the necessary identification with the object in order to close the circle. This is *kinbaku-bi,* the "beauty of tight binding." From the standpoint of the one being bound, the technique of kinbaku can facilitate trancelike states leading to inner liberation. Kinbaku can be a mode of sensory deprivation or a way to cause continuous pain.

Techniques of Japanese rope bondage have been making their ways into the Western practice of Sado-Masochistic sexuality for many decades. Although there may *appear* to be many similarities between Japanese and Western traditions of Sado-Masochism, on an inner cultural and psychological level the *differences* are often profound and fascinating. For some of the information in this section, we are indebted to the guidance of Master "K."

There have been several personalities in modern European and American history who have greatly influenced our perceptions of this kind of sexuality. The two most famous are the Marquis de Sade and Leopold von Sacher-Masoch. Each of whom deserves some attention here.

THE MARQUIS DE SADE

Dontien Alphonse François Marquis de Sade (1740–1814) was philosophically a radical materialist, and so he is quite atypical of "magicians" as we usually expect to find them. But magic can often be found in the most unexpected places.

As a materialist de Sade was following his countryman Julien Offray de la Mettrie (1709–1752), who was in turn following the philosophy of the ancient Epicureans who held that all that existed was made up of material atoms—including what most call the soul or spirit.

De Sade is hardly the writer of "pornography" he is popularly held to be. His works are, by far, more full of questions of cosmology, theology, and psychology than they are of sex.

Georges Bataille, who also cites the work of Maurice Blanchot, refers to de Sade's philosophy as one that extols the absolute sovereignty of the individual who exists in solitude, apart from other individuals whom he does not recognize as his equals. Other humans exist for his pleasure alone—to be his victims. In this de Sade denies the basic precepts of the Reason of his day, and gives vent to a pure "bestial" nature devoid of Reason. In this limitless world of isolate subjective imaginings, which the Sadist attempts to impose upon the world of men around him, the Sadist derives his pleasure. Bataille also eloquently points out that, in fact, de Sade's refined use of language, which indicates the Marquis' awareness of his imagined cruelties, actually precludes his actual criminality: violence is silent and dumb, eloquent thoughts and words are incompatible with actual violence. This is perhaps at the root of why and how Sadeans are the least violent of people, in fact.

Julius Evola, in his *Metaphysics of Sex* (pp. 105–12), identifies aspects of de Sade's philosophy with Eastern forms of the left-hand path, or *vamachara*. According to Evola the vamachara emphasizes the destruction of order, norms, and laws—and de Sade is doing the same in his philosophy. The left-hand path aspects of de Sade's ideas are further explored in *Lords of the Left-Hand Path* (pp. 165–70).

The human faculty of imagination is the key to de Sade's psychology. De Sade writes in *Justine, Philosophy of the Bedroom and*

Other Writings, "Imagination is pleasure's spur . . . directs every-thing, is the motive for everything; is it not thence that our pleasure comes?"[1] Here his ideas concerning the erotic enter his philosophy most directly. De Sade says that the pursuit of pleasure is the object of human life, and that physical satisfaction is more noble than the merely mental. Happiness depends on the greatest possible exten-sion of pleasure. This is done by enlarging the scope of one's tastes and fantasies. Only through willful imagination can the possibili-ties for pleasure be extended. Social or religious conditioning pre-vents most people from fulfilling themselves in this way.

De Sade says there are essentially three kinds of people when it comes to eroticism: 1) those of weak or repressed imagination, courage and desires—and who live without remarkable incident; 2) "natural perverts"—who act out of obsession, which is usually congenital in origin, and 3) libertines—who consciously develop their fantasies and who set about to realize them. This third cat-egory, the Libertines, by actively using their imaginations, trans-form themselves through acts of will, as de Sade would have it, "in accordance with Nature." This is the key to the magical use of de Sade's ideas.

Whether in the sexual or more abstract philosophical sphere, social anthropologist Geoffrey Gorer provides the truest defini-tion of Sadeanism: "The pleasure felt from the observed modifica-tion on the external world produced by the will of the observer."

The legacy of de Sade has really been more a matter of aes-thetic reputation than a true understanding of his philosophy. Only certain limited aspects of that philosophy are generally accepted by postmodern Sadeans, although de Sade is acknowl-edged as the modern founder of the theoretical basis of the con-scious experience of this type of sexuality.

LEOPOLD RITTER VON SACHER-MASOCH

Leopold von Sacher-Masoch (1835–1895) was born into a family of the Austro-Hungarian petty nobility. His father was chief of police in Lemberg, Austria. Leopold highly identified with the agrarian, semipagan sects of the Slavs of Galatia and idealized the almost savage "Sarmatian" woman. In the early part of Masoch's career as an author he was well respected for his literary achievements. These were only later in his lifetime to be stigmatized by pathologizing professors of the *belles lettres.*

When Masoch was just ten years old he had an experience that was to leave a lasting imprint on his soul. One Sunday afternoon, when the young Leopold was visiting the house of his "aunt-in-law," the Countess Zenobia, he was asked to help her take off her sable cloak and put on her squirrel-lined green velvet jacket, all of which gave him a surge of erotic feeling. Later, while Leopold was hiding in her boudoir, this aunt received a young suitor as the youngster watched in terror of being discovered. He witnessed the countess being confronted by her husband, whom she then beat with a whip. Moments later he was discovered, whereupon Leopold reports that she "seized me by the hair and threw me to the carpet; she then placed her knee upon my shoulder and began to whip me vigorously. . . . And yet I must admit that while I writhed under my aunt's cruel blows, I experienced acute pleasure."[2]

Masoch's continual replaying of aspects of this scene in his erotic life and literary imagination is a manifestation of what might be called "imprinting." Such imprinting goes beyond mere pleasurable recollections and may play a role in conserving actual life force by restimulating psychophysiological channels in the organism.

I am highly indebted to the work of Gilles Deleuze for my understanding of the work of Masoch. For while the often ponderous works of the Marquis de Sade have all been translated into English, it seems that the usually more literarily meritorious works of Masoch have been largely ignored by publishers, literary critics, and translators.

Masoch's literary vision was to create a cycle of works he called *The Heritage of Cain*. Only two of the projected six works were ever completed—*The Divorced Woman* and his most famous book, *Venus in Furs*—both published in 1870. These and other of his novels and short stories reveal some of the scope of his vision, however. Although not as explicit and philosophical as de Sade, Masoch, too, was interested in matters of politics and religion. Masoch, like de Sade, was a nobleman with an interest in the rights of the common man, or peasantry. Almost all of Masoch's stories have as a theme the exercise of tyrannical power (of an eastern European noblewoman) over members of the local peasantry. This exercise of power is ambiguously viewed by Masoch with a combination of lust and horror.

Although the Marquis de Sade has lent his name more prominently to the theory and practice of this form of sexuality, it is perhaps Sacher-Masoch who was really the father of what we call the D/S or S/M movement in human sexuality in this century. The actual works of Sade are filled with things that most "Sadeans" of today find abhorrent. This is chiefly because in Sade's works pain and bondage are almost always inflicted non-consensually. The Sadist (as opposed to the Sadean) derives pleasure from breaking contracts—the Masochist is virtually obsessed with making them.

In reality the ideologies expounded by Sade and Masoch are not two ends of the same spectrum or continuum. They were analysed as belonging to such a spectrum by the German psychopathologist Richard Freiherr von Krafft-Ebing (in his *Psychopathia Sexualis*). However, this does not make the analysis correct.

In fact what seems to have happened is that the "safe, sane, consensual" tradition of Sado-Masochistic sexuality is an expression of what Masoch was talking about, while the all-too-common "dangerous and coercive" tradition is closer to the truth of Sade's philosophy. Strictly speaking we have Sadism (with an active and passive role of behavior). For the sake of simplicity (and for aesthetic reasons as well) we choose to call the active Masochist a Sadean and only the passive Masochist by that name.

Deleuze astutely analyzes the transformative and even initiatory qualities of Masoch's work.

The masochistic contract generates a type of law that leads straight to ritual. The masochist is obsessed; ritualistic activity is essential to him, since it epitomizes the world of fantasy. Three main types of rite occur in Masoch's novels: hunting rites, agricultural rites, and rites of regeneration and rebirth. They echo the three fundamental elements: cold, that requires the conquest of the fur, the trophy of the hunt; the buried sentimentality and sheltered fecundity, which agriculture demands, together with the strictest organization of work; and finally that very element of strictness, that cruel rigor which regeneration and rebirth demand. The coexistence and interaction of these three rites sum up the mystical complex of masochism. We find it again and again, variously embodied throughout the work of Masoch: the ideal woman hunts the bear or the wolf; she organizes or presides over an agricultural community; she makes man undergo a process of rebirth.[3]

It is unfortunate that Sacher-Masoch's contemporary literary reputation was ruined by having his name attached to a "sexual pathology." Perhaps we can do something to repair his reputation, not by disassociating him from this form of sexuality, but by providing greater understanding for the sexual format itself, and the symbolic use of explicit sexuality in literature.

*   *

*

Some of the best known names in the "magical revival" of the early part of the twentieth century have been involved with the practice of Sado-Magic personally, although often their public writings did not make this explicit.

ALEISTER CROWLEY

In the modern history of sexual magic no one has been more influential than Aleister Crowley (1875–1947). His influence stems from the fact that he wrote so much, and so well, and that he founded or reformed at least two important magical organizations.

Crowley's father was a wealthy brewer and member of a fundamentalist Christian sect known as "the Plymouth Brethren." His father died in 1886, and Crowley's future exploits were largely financed through his inheritance. As a young man his avocations were poetry and mountain climbing. In December 1896, while in Stockholm, he began to realize the possibilities of magical philosophy. Two years later he entered the "Hermetic Order of the Golden Dawn." By 1900 he was initiated to the Adeptus Minor grade in that order, but not long after this he was alienated from the organization and began an independent career in magical studies.

In 1904 Crowley conducted a magical working in Cairo, Egypt, in which he received the words of a text entitled *Liber Al vel Legis: The Book of the Law* from a discarnate entity calling itself "Aiwaz." In 1907 he founded his own order, the Argentum Astrum (Silver Star).

Apparently the A∴ A∴ did not fulfill every possible magical function since Crowley subsequently undertook an alliance with a pseudo-Masonic German lodge—the Ordo Templi Orientis—in 1912. This order taught forms of sexual magic akin to Indian tantrism. Crowley was absorbed in this kind of magic for the rest of his life.

Crowley died in relative obscurity in Hastings, England, on December 1, 1947, in the fullness of seventy-two years of age. But his philosophy has remained influential throughout the Western magical world during the latter half of the twentieth century.

Although Crowley is perhaps best known for his sexual magic, he published very little that dealt with the subject in any specific way. What he did publish was often in veiled terms or a "twilight language." Later interpreters and disciples have made explicit what Crowley only hinted at in his own lifetime. But Crowley is very explicit (even if often couched in cryptic magical shorthand) in his personal magical diaries. These were not published until after his death. In these diaries we not only see the manner of his working of sexual magic in general, but the extent to which Sadean sexuality played a part in it.

From an early age Crowley displayed an interest in Sado-Masochistic sexuality—especially with himself as the submissive. This matured into a magical interest by 1920. Diary entries during the summer of that year, written while Crowley and his followers were at the "Abby of Thelema" near Cefalu in Sicily, reveal the depth and nature of his Masochistic workings. As we will discuss in chapter 4, it should not come as a surprise that this dominant magical personality would gravitate toward the submissive role in Sado-Magic. This is because the magician Crowley seems to have been primarily interested in self-transformation, in the transformation of his own subjective universe, and the submissive role is the most direct route to this goal.

Crowley's Sado-Magical technique is clear from his diary entries of June 18 and July 22 and 26. These entries also testify to the intensity of these workings. Here we can only outline some of the aspects of these workings, which are more complex than we have space to enter into here. As discussed in chapter 4 of this book, the Masochistic, or submissive, Sado-Shaman projects ideal qualities onto his partner, who embodies those qualities. Then through his or her domination and enslaving of the submissive the Masochistic Sado-Shaman is imprinted with the willed ideal qualities. Subjective transformation is achieved.

In Crowley's diary entry of June 18, 1920, we read:

I drown in delight at the thought that I who have been Master of the Universe should lie beneath Her feet, Her slave, Her victim, eager to be abased, passionately a thirst for suffering, swooning at Her cruelty, craving Her contempt; 'tis joy to be splashed with the mire of Her Triumph, to bleed under the whip's lash, to choke as Her heel treads my throat . . .

Here the magician clearly attains a higher state of consciousness by submitting his Mastery to the envisioned higher Being of Her.

In the entry of July 22 the extended magical working has progressed to the point where he writes:

[1:45 a.m.] . . . I swore to take Her as my High Priestess to Him [Crowley's personal god, Aiwaz] and act accordingly. She is to direct all action, and taking the initiative throughout.

[4:00 a.m.] We have been continuing Cocaine in a Lesbian Orgie in which I was Alys, her tribade, after a frightful ordeal of cruelty and defilement put on me as her fist passion for Her slave, which tore from me the last rag of manhood, violated my last veil of modesty . . .

It was for her to Nurse Her Babe, train it with Her sharp whips and sharper words, bring it to puberty, to virile might, and . . . murder him in his Father's House . . . Fling him Her Satan into the Bottomless Pit [the vulva] . . .whence first he issued to those stupid wanderings that naught could end but their own homecoming.

The workings of this night conclude with Crowley being forced to lick the feet of his Scarlet Woman.

In the course of these magical experiences the magician envisions himself being magically transformed into a woman, symbolically slain, and resurrected by Her, and eventually gains union with Her as a whole Being.

This series of Workings ultimately concludes with the extensive entry of July 26 in which we learn that he has had to endure being burned with lighted cigarettes and forced into an act of coprophagy as a kind of Holy Eucharist.

Undoubtedly Aleister Crowley was a pansexual satyrist who left no aspect of sexuality unexplored for its magical potentials—and certainly did not neglect the "English vice."

ERNST SCHERTEL

The Philosopher King of Weimar Germany, as he was called by Mel Gordon, was born in Munich in 1884 and died in relative obscurity in Hof in 1958. The peak of his artistic, scholarly, and philosophical career came in the years leading up to the Nazi assumption of power in Germany at the beginning of 1933.

Early in life Schertel was tormented by crushing inhibitions. His inner life of imagination was wild and sensual, but he could not express this part of himself for fear of eternal damnation. He received a Ph.D. in philosophy at Jena in 1911. In the summer of 1912 he began writing a semiautobiographical "gnostic" novel entitled *Die Sünde des Ewigen: Dies ist mein Leib* ("The Sin of Eternity: This is my Body"). The effects of this writing process, finished in 1913, were magically liberating. He says of himself after completing the work: "I threw myself into life like an unchained predatory beast, without inhibition, in a frenzy of enjoyment and real action."

After spending a few years as a teacher in a progressive college preparatory school, where he organized the students in dance performances he called "Mystery Plays," Schertel began a career as an author, lecturer, teacher of dance, and publicist. He became ever more successful in these endeavors, publishing works on nudism, occultism, the history of culture as it relates to the expression of primal urges and instincts, and his favorite topic, the art and literature of Sado-Masochistic sexuality.

His masterpiece is generally acknowledged to be *Der*

Flagellantismus als literarisches Motiv ("Flagellation as a Literary Motif") [in 4 volumes, 1929–1932]. More recently he has also generated some attention because of his book on occultism entitled *Magie* ("Magic"), which he sent to the voracious reader and charismatic, yet upstart, political organizer, Adolf Hitler, in 1923. Schertel had no real sympathy for the Nazis in general and was, in fact, later persecuted and imprisoned by them. His books were banned, and he was stripped of his Ph.D. in 1937 by Nazi authorities.

After the war Schertel recovered enough to begin to try to reissue some of his old material—but postwar Germany was not the same freewheeling world of intra-war Berlin. Just before his death he was able to republish his masterpiece under the new title *Der Flagellantismus in Literature und Bildnerei* (1957).

Dr. Ernst Schertel must be considered the grandfather of Carnal Alchemy. His worldview was dominated by the triad of eroticism, magic, and Sado-Masochism. As much as Schertel wrote, nowhere did he entirely betray the secrets of his own *personal* work and activities.

The essence of Schertel's magical theory is that powerful and unique personalities could be developed through techniques designed to dissolve the ordinarily perceived distinctions between the "body" and the "spirit," between the "real" and the "ideal." These integrative processes hinged on techniques of corporeal experience—eroticism, nudity, indulgence in exhibitionism, and voyeurism, unconventional "dance" movements, pleasure, and pain.

WILLIAM SEABROOK

We are indebted to the pioneering work in original scholarship done by Robert North, the late Visible Head of the New Flesh

Palladium, for making us aware of Seabrook's experiments with Sado-Shamanism. Some of this experimental work is contained in the third part of Seabrook's classic study *Witchcraft: Its Power in the World Today* (1940).

Seabrook was a writer, a journalist, and an adventurer who explored the inner and outer landscapes of Asia, Africa, and Haiti. In the early 1930s he spent time in Paris, where he became part of the circle surrounding Maria de Naglowska. Naglowska's circle is also said to have included Jean Paulhan, for whom Dominique Aury (Pauline Réage) wrote *Story of O*. One of the rites of the system practiced by Maria de Naglowska involved the short but actual hanging of a male initiate before engaging in an act of sexual magic with an officiating priestess.

Seabrook also lived for some years in New York City and in the Hudson Valley town of Rhinebeck, where he carried out experiments in what was just then being called E.S.P. and its links to the techniques usually associated with bondage and discipline. Two of these experiments, carried out with the aid of a woman he calls "Justine," involved prolonged suspension and sensory deprivation by means of what might be called a bondage or discipline hood. These experiments were conducted in the years just prior to the Second World War.

In the method Seabrook called "Dervish Dangling" Justine would be suspended by a rope with straps around her wrists. She would stand on tiptoe supported by telephone books. If the rope became lax, she could restore or increase the tension by moving one or more of the books out from under her feet. She would dangle in darkness for several hours at a time—and on occasion she would actually be able to go "through a 'slit'" or "through a 'door'" into another "world in time-space, beyond our three-dimensional horizon . . ." On one occasion Justine was able to foresee accurately an experience she would share with Willie some months later in the southern French city of Avignon. This involved an unlikely set of events surrounding a lady lion tamer and an old lion pissing on the audience.

The other technique was the use of a leather mask, sometimes called the *caput mortuum,* which effectively cuts off all sensory input from the eyes, nose, and ears, as well as eliminating otherwise dominant tactile input from the skin on the face. Seabrook reports that at first Justine "feared and hated" wearing the mask, but eventually she grew to like it. Justine would also be bound in various postures to reduce other sensory data, especially to reduce input from the hands. Her most dramatic success with this method was when she foresaw that her cousin would receive an unlikely delivery of a "barrel of fish." This indeed did happen some months later.

These and other similar activities were entered into by Seabrook and those who worked with him in the spirit of experimental games—half scientific, half erotic play. This may be the key to their rate of success.

GERALD GARDNER

Gerald Brosseau Gardner (1884–1964) was a man of little formal education who spent most of his adult life in the Far East. He retired from the commercial branch of the British Civil Service in 1936 when he returned to England and slowly began to create the religious system now known as "Wicca." No one can read anything about Gardner's original system of initiation and magic and not be impressed with the amount of whipping and bondage involved. Some have even been prompted to speculate that he invented the system to satisfy his own sexual needs! Historical and personal facts speak to the reality that he had (by his own nature and predispositions) tapped into a legitimate and powerful way of working magic: one with deep roots in his English ancestry.

This world of traditional magical flagellation and bondage in the context of European witchcraft has most recently been explored on a practical level by Inga Steddinger in her volume titled *Wiccan Sex-Magic*.

Initiations into "Gardnerian Witchcraft" involve binding the initiate to an altar and scourging him or her with a whip. Thereafter he or she gives the presiding Priestess or Priest (always of the opposite sex from the initiate) a "fivefold kiss"—upon the feet, knees, genitals, breast, and mouth. This is really a classic manifestation of the ritualism of Sado-Magic.

A revealing example of how Gardner practiced Sado-Magic is illustrated in a text, which he left behind in his own "Book of Shadows." It is printed here verbatim as edited by Aidan Kelly in his groundbreaking piece of research titled *Crafting the Art of Magic* (St. Paul: Llewellyn, 1991).

> *(Feet , knees, and wrists should be tightly bound*
> *to retard blood.) Scourge 40 or more, to make*
> *skin tingle, then say, invoking Goddess,*
> *Hail, Aradia, from the Amalthean horn*
> *Pour forth thy store of Love. Lowly I bend*
> *Before thee! I invoke thee at the end*
> *When other Gods are fallen and put to scorn.*
> *Thy foot to my lips! My sighs inborn*

Rise, touch, curl about thy heart. Then spend,
Pitiful Love, loveliest Pity, descend
And bring me luck who am lonely and forlorn.[4]*

Ask the Goddess to help you obtain your desires, then Scourge again to bind the spell. This will be powerful in ill luck and for sickness. It must be said in a Circle, and you must be properly prepared and well purified, both before and after saying, to bind the spell.

Before starting you must make a very clear picture in your mind of what you wish. Make yourself see the wish obtained. Be sure in your own mind exactly what it is and how it is to be fulfilled. This spell is the one that was taught to me long ago, and I have found it works, but I don't think there is any special virtue in the words. Any others can be substituted provided they ask the goddess's (or god's) help and say clearly what you wish and you form the clear mental image; and if it doesn't work at first, keep on trying until it works. Your helper, who wields the scourge, must know what you wish and also from the mental image. And at first, at any rate, it will be better for you to work the spell, then for the girl to take your place and work it also; you scourge her. Don't try anything difficult at first, and do it at least once a week until it works. You have to get into sympathy with each other, before anything happens, and regular Working helps this.

A knowledgeable reading of this "spell" reveals a sorcerer who was very familiar with the magical workings of S-M. In reality he makes us privy to the essence of his type of Sado-Magic. Notice

---

*This poem by W. E. Henley, from vol. III of his *Rodin in Rime* (p. 20) is cited by J. F. C. Fuller in his study of the poetry of Aleister Crowley (*The Star in the West* [1907], pp. 37–38), which is doubtless Gardner's source for it.

that it begins with bondage, then goes on to flagellation, during which time the flagellant focuses his or her imagination on the desired result—but in a sacralized, prayerful, and submissive mood. Gardner makes it clear that the power is in the actions, not in the words of the "spell." Finally he is keenly aware that the dominant and the submissive must be in "sympathy with each other before anything happens."

The whole movement of modern "Wicca," which now encompasses the spiritual lives of hundreds of thousands of people around the world, had its genesis in the magical Workings of Mr. Gardner. The essence of his magical technique was obviously Sadean. Sadly this Sadean element is often the first aspect to be eliminated from his system by more "politically correct" modern Wiccans who are often likely to view it as some sort of an "embarrassment." By doing this they trade true and authentic magical power for political expediency. As Gardner says of the flagellant rite above: "This is the one that was taught to me long ago, and I have found that it works . . ."[5] However he came by his knowledge of Sado-Magic, he seems to have applied it well. This aspect is especially pursued—if secretly—by the branch of witchcraft known as Vana-Troth.

ANTON SZANDOR LAVEY

Anton LaVey (1930–1997) was a self-made *myth* of a man. In 1966 he founded the Church of Satan, which was in its earliest days best known for its nude female altars and apparently orgiastic goings-on in LaVey's "Black House" at 6114 California Street in San Francisco. Some of the images of LaVey's early Church of Satan rituals include LaVey spanking one of his "topless witches" and one gentleman in bishop's vestments being flagellated. LaVey was a close friend of the famous Dutch dominatrix Monique van Cleef—who was said to be a Priestess in his Church. But LaVey's interest in the magical philosophy of S-M went well beyond these provocative facts and images.

A serious study of LaVey's views reveals a materialistic philosophy very much akin to that held by the Marquis de Sade himself. LaVey's worldview revolved around social dynamics, especially as these relate to the relationship between the sexes. The magic he saw in all this involves the exchange of power and the increase of mutual power between individuals. LaVey always saw a question of dominance and submission in the relationship between the sexes or between any two individual humans. One will dominate the other, one will be the master, the other the slave. He was also quick to point out that there is power to be gained in being the slave as well—it all depends on the nature of the master and what the slave gets in exchange for her (or his) slavery.

LaVey believed that masochistic tendencies can begin in the phenomenon of "eustress"—or "good-stress" (as opposed to distress = "bad-stress"). People love to suffer fear and pain—think of all the recreational activities based on experiencing these things— from horror movies to roller coaster rides, and from aerobics classes to dieting—people will even pay good money to suffer fear and pain. They need it, they have to have it, they won't be happy without it. "No pain, no gain!"

He even went so far as to say that inherent masochism is the major factor in marketing products. The name of the game is increasing consumer anxiety and dissatisfaction (= pain). The consumer is led to believe that he or she can only "spell relief" by buying the products or participating in the popular consumer trends—all of which LaVey cynically pointed out are inherently "painful" (physically, emotionally, or financially).

The magic here comes through a certain psychological mechanism. Some elements of mankind (and according to LaVey especially womankind!) need a certain amount of misery, pain, and slavery. This inherent need will be played out in life one way or another. Because most people are unconscious of this need in themselves it simply gets played out in unhappy circumstances of life. This becomes what LaVey called "self-destructive masochism."[6] Actual misfortune and misery are the only result. But if one is a "self-affirming masochist," who is conscious of this element in the personality, and who lives it out in a creative and self-aware manner, then the actual misery can be "exorcised" in a pleasurable and fun way.

Typically unaware or unconscious Masochists are people for whom "everything seems to go wrong." They have lousy jobs, can't get dates, their cars are always breaking down. Misery follows them wherever they go, and they are unhappy. Such persons are probably Masochists who are unaware of their needs. Various aspects of the objective universe, however, provide for them in most unpleasant and miserable ways. If these same Masochists discover the true nature of these needs, and play them out in real but controlled (and often ritualized) ways, the real-life miseries will be banished and replaced by fun and pleasurable indulgences in slavery and torture! The Masochist will have a Master (or Mistress). The self-aware Masochist can simply choose one of his or her taste.

LaVey's ideas about Sadism were also interesting. He thought of the Sadist as a facilitator of the self-aware Masochist's experience. In the relationship between the Sadist and the Masochist there is a true exchange of power in which both give something and both gain something they inherently need. There is also the recognition that the roots of the true Sadistic impulse lie not in hatred or anger, but in jealousy or envy. The Masochist is viewed as a projection of the Sadist's own inner or, as he called it, "demonic" self. The Sadist then proceeds to train, control, and even punish a symbol of his or her "demonic self" through the Masochist.

The Sadist is also the Artist. The insightful definition of Sadeanism offered by Gorer ("the pleasure felt from the observed modifications on the external world produced by the will of the observer"[7]) is equally true of the Artist or Magician. In the work of all of these types something is imagined in the subjective universe and from there it is caused to come into being in the objective universe.

These ideas recall the Greek myth of the misogynistic Pygmalion who created the sculpture of Galatea—his perfect woman. But in an ironic twist he then fell in love with her—even though her stony form was unreceptive to his love. The goddess of love, Aphrodite, took pity on Pygmalion and caused the sculpture to take on a fleshly form that could be his wife. (This is the origin of the story of Henry Higgins and Eliza Dolittle by way of George Bernard Shaw's *Pygmalion*.)

Here we are also reminded of what Michelangelo said of the marble from which he sculpted his great works such as *David* or the *Pietà*. He held that the shapes were already hiding in the marble, and that his work was to liberate them. He could only transform marble from a cold and hard substance into something warm, supple, and endowed with spirit if the marble wanted to be so transformed. The true Sadist works with the same attitude as

Michelangelo. The Masochistic need must, in fact, dwell in the heart of the Slave before the Sadist can bring it out.

Two contemporary magical orders either dedicated to or heavily influenced by Sado-Magic are the New Flesh Palladium and the now retired Order of the Triskelion.

THE NEW FLESH PALLADIUM AND ROBERT NORTH

Robert North was the Grand Imperial Hierophant of the New Flesh Palladium and Visible Head of that Order. The New Flesh Palladium traces its roots to the nineteenth-century organizations known as the "Re-Theurgists Optimates" and the "Hermetic Brotherhood of Luxor." The NFP surfaced in the late twentieth century in such places as St. Charles, Missouri; Key West, Florida; Providence, Rhode Island; and Lyon, France. It was first headquartered in Boston, Massachusetts, home of Paschal Beverly Randolph's Brotherhood of Eulis a hundred years earlier and later in Miami, Florida. Robert North was best known to the public for his translation and biography of P. B. Randolph titled *Sexual Magic*. His other writings included *The New Flesh Palladium: Magica Erotica* (1996) and "Maria Naglowska: The Satanic Woman" (1993) later incorporated in *The Magical Grimoire of Maria Naglowska* (2009).

The wisdom that "God is Man, Man is God" is the primary postulate of the NFP. The magick of the New Flesh is defined as the employment of supersensual techniques to empower self and escape alienation, or on a more technical note, to accumulation and manipulation of sexual energy in its most extreme forms. Within the order teachings there are seven sacraments that the New Flesh refers to:

(1) The Creole expression "Wete Po, Mete Po," to remove the skin to put on new skin. This is a key phrase and concept in the secret Bizango societies of Haiti, who trace their spiritual lineage back to the ancient Obeah cults of primal Africa.

(2) A Tibetan yogic meditation, probably from the ancient Bön religion, visualizes the flesh melting away from the bones of the yogi, leaving only the skeleton. New Flesh is then seen to flower from the bones to create a perfect body of light.

(3) The sexual fluids of the male and female and the mingling thereof, which, according to occult doctrine, inevitably creates new life, either on the material or the astral plane.

(4) The addition of encumberments, masks, restraints, and other bondage devices to the flesh.

(5) The new skin that grows as the result of the scarification rites that are considered an essential preliminary to spirit possession in many shamanistic cults.

(6) The doctrine of New Life and inner respiration taught by Thomas Lake Harris.

(7) Surgical procedures for sexual regeneration to restore dormant sexual organs thereby returning man to his original, pre-Adamite, physical bisexuality.

The central ritual of the NFP is Oscar Wilde's *Salomé* performed in a sexually explicit manner. Elements of sensory deprivation, Sado-Masochism, and ritual magick are key components. Membership in the Palladium is never divulged to the public, and admittance is by invitation only.

The parent organization of the New Flesh was considered to be the Brotherhood of *La Fleche d'Or*, the Golden Arrow. This was founded by Maria de Naglowska, who flourished in 1930s Paris, where she became notorious for celebrating her "Mass of Gold" and proclaiming "Satanic Initiation according to the Third Term of the Trinity." Robert North did pioneering research on her from the early 1990s. Her teachings focused on a sacred sexuality whereby "the priestesses of love are destined to prepare the future of humanity." Although she only recently has become known to the English-speaking world, her disciples included French writers Michel Leiris, Georges Bataille, and Pierre Klossowski, as well as Jean Paulhan, the writer who inspired *Story of O*. She also included among her Brotherhood of the Golden Arrow the adventurer William B. Seabrook, whose experiments with S-M and E.S.P. were the scandal of Paris.

The New Flesh teachings are heavily influenced by Symbolist and Surrealist doctrines. The Palladist is expected to go through such ordeals as "entering the body of Babylon," engaging in the "six modes of congress," performing the "sex mutation" and enduring the ordeal of the "mystery of the Hanging." This is Strong Medicine, which includes explicit instructions regarding blood sacrifice, bondage, the whip, right use of sexual fluids, drug-induced ecstasies, and other aspects of the magickal tradition, which can only be communicated from mouth to ear.

THE ORDER OF THE TRISKELION

Sado-Shamanism and Carnal Alchemy are basically our own coinages. One of the authors of this book, Stephen Flowers, also writes and is known under the name Edred Thorsson. He was the Grand Master of the Order of the Triskelion, which is currently closed. The basic information letter of the Order appears as an appendix to this book for historical purposes. Elements of Sado-Shamanism are to be found in various parts of his published work, although it is not present everywhere. Some esoteric teachings of the Rune-Gild may include the secrets of polarian mysteries of the Norse God Odin closely related to the operating principles of Sado-Shamanism.

Stephen received his early training in the world of Sadeanism when he was introduced to it as a young man while studying in Germany in the early 1970s. His mentors were members of the *Burggesellschaft,* or "Chateau Society." In the 1980s he founded and developed the Order of the Triskelion in this country based on his experiences.

Besides the work of the Triskelion, Stephen has developed and experimented with a variety of magical and initiatory techniques within the Gothic and Witchcraft traditions.

Underlying all of his work in these fields is his idea of transformation through the synthesis of polar extremes, such as pain and pleasure, bondage and liberation, humiliation and pride, along with that experienced between the selves of the (empowered) dominant and (powerless) submissive, which, when combined with a Sense of Mystery, of voyaging into the Unknown, result in the formula that leads to personal transformation. The transmutation of one polar extreme to another is the essence of what is called "Carnal Alchemy."

Another of Stephen's contributions to the field of operative Sadeanism was what he called the "Triskelion Process." This was a part of the curriculum of the Order of the Triskelion and cannot be entered into here in too much detail. It is experienced in the form of layer upon layer of Mystery, guided by an initiated Master or Mistress. In many ways the Triskelion Process is a magical formula for the conscious articulation and/or generation of fantasies of a Sadean nature, the conscious desire to fulfill these fantasies, and finally the experience of the fantasy in the flesh. Once this pattern of the "fleshing of fantasy" has been actualized often enough in the context of the chamber, its power inevitably manifests in other aspects of the initiate's life. The Triskelion Process has been called a mechanism for "making dreams come true."

In 1990 Stephen met his eternal lover, Crystal Dawn, who subsequently became the Grand Mistress of the Order of the Triskelion and was the leader of the Onyx Circle under the sponsorship of the Order.

*　　　*
*

Only in the latter part of the twentieth century did the full magical and spiritual implications of the practice of the techniques discussed in this book again become manifest in European culture. It is part of our ancient heritage, and it is part of the continuing heritage of many other peoples, but it has been, and will continue to be, for pioneers of the present to rediscover the mysteries of the past and to create other horizons yet Unknown.

3
GENERAL THEORY OF CARNAL ALCHEMY AND SADO-MAGIC

All of the theories and "laws" pertaining to the practice of sexual magic in general apply to the practice of Carnal Alchemy. However, Sado-Magic takes these theories and ideas a few steps further. Most obviously, Sado-Magical techniques could be employed to deepen levels of sexual excitement in individuals oriented toward this kind of eroticism. This is empowering according to the general rule: "The higher the level of arousal, the more sexual energy the magician has to work with."

Beyond this, however, there are magical—physiological and spiritual—aspects to which only "Strong Medicine," to use Robert North's term, can give access. This is due to the fact that only in S-M sexuality are all of the human potentials for extreme polarities of psychosensual experience present and manifest.

In the realm of theory this is manifest in the two poles of the sources of power in Sado-Shamanism: the physiological and semiotic or symbolic. The physiological pole is focused on the actual physical, somatic (body-centered), chemical processes, alterations, and manipulations, which are caused to occur in the participants. This pole of the theory underscores such somatic mechanisms as the production of endorphins through painful stimuli, the physiological effects of prolonged physical stress, sensory deprivation, and so on—always in conjunction with sexual or erotic excitement. The presence of the erotic dimension clearly separates this type of shamanism from all others. Here again are keys to what is called "Carnal Alchemy."

Alchemy is the spiritual or magical discipline in which chemical or metallurgical processes are carried out in an analogical relationship to inner transformations. Alchemy is best known for its promise to hold the secret to the philosophers' stone by which the alchemist could transform lead into gold. By analogy, "Carnal

Alchemy" can transform pain into pleasure, powerlessness into empowerment.

Some might argue that the only "real" level of power is contained in these physiological processes. But the human being is a spiritual "animal," the symbol-making animal, who can only exist in a world of symbolic culture. This is why, for real transformations to take place, the symbolic pole of the theory of Sado-Shamanism cannot be ignored.

With the physiological aspect of the theory we remain on fairly predictable ground. There is only one basic "chemistry" of the human body, and so methods of manipulating that chemistry can be fairly well understood in a universal way. This is not true of the semiotic or symbolic level. In this world, quite to the contrary of the physiological world, every individual system is in some way different and unique.

In fact, as all who have experienced these forms of sexuality can probably attest, the act of even playing games of bondage and discipline requires that there be an ongoing synthesis between the body-level experience and the head-level experience, between the body game and the head game. This must be so for the scene to "work." This experience is the beginning of the understanding of what Sado-Magic is all about.

In our times the "head game," the symbolic game, seems to be played out on two significant levels: the psychological and the social. Many are again becoming comfortable calling the psychological realm "spiritual" (which it really is) while others might insist that the social aspect is really more political. In this last regard we are speaking in terms of what might be called "sexual politics." Postmodern Western society has become obsessed with the relationship between the sexes, and the ratio of power vested in the symbolism of the two sexes. As Carnal Alchemy is a system concerned with power and the exchange of power in symbolic and actual carnal ways, it may hold a key to the transformation of not only individual bodies and souls but also of whole segments of our society as well.

Essential to how alchemy works, how base things are transformed into nobler things, it is the process technically known as *solve et coagula*—a Latin phrase that implies "breaking down into component parts and recombining them in a new and more perfect form." In Carnal Alchemy every time the submissive is "broken down," humiliated, caused to submit to the power of the dominant, he or she is made the object of transformation into a more "perfect" being. The broken down elements are recombined in a more ideal form. This is the essence of "training."

By the way, this mode of working is, in fact, the way in which such things are done. This is why the would-be Marine is broken down, dehumanized, crushed—both physically and mentally—so that he can be recombined (physically and mentally) into what the Marine Corps wants a Marine to be. This is true of monastic orders, and many other institutions in which profound personal transformation is essential.

The total theory of Carnal Alchemy only becomes clear after a certain degree of practice has been engaged in. The essential transformative secret of this lies in the proper use of the Fire: sexual excitement and orgasm. This is the element used to fix the coagulated state in the submissive.

We will also come back to this alchemical model to illustrate points in chapters 4 and 5. With the ancient formula of solve et coagula all kinds of transformations and transmutations are possible.

Perhaps the greatest power of Carnal Alchemy lies in the depth of the reality of the polarities being used. There is nothing more fundamental to basic human existence than the experience of the difference between pleasure and pain, no realization more profound than the dichotomy between the self and not-self of the world, or, in a subjective reflection of that dichotomy, the difference between one's own body and one's own mind (or spirit). Carnal Alchemy takes these most fundamental of polar opposites and endeavors to transmute one into the other—all the while in a conscious state. To do this a third term is necessary. This third term is a Mystery. Some call it "God," others "a god," still others "the Principle of Isolate Intelligence." The point is that there exists a "higher power," the exact character of which remains categorically Unknown to us. Into the darkness of the Unknown we have room to grow.

A basic element of sexual magic in general, and one that is even more pronounced in the practice of all forms of Sado-Magic, is the "deification" of the partner in the subjective universe—in the mind's eye—of each participant. In tantrism the man invokes "the Goddess" in the woman and the woman invokes "the God" in the man. This is easy to see in the way the submissive sees the dominant. The submissive wants to view the dominant as a God/dess-like ideal, and this vision can be of great psychological benefit in the actual performance of the rites of Sado-Magic. But it is equally true that the dominant must be able to see in the submissive an equally divine quality. To the dominant, however, the divinity of the submissive is that inherent in Nature, or that which is seen as the eternal "Other," which is always sought but rarely found. By seeing the Divine in each other both the dominant and submissive come to discover more precisely the Divine within themselves—not through abstract meditation but through carnal experience.

The fundamental polarities inherent in Carnal Alchemy are reflected in its theory: it works with those things, which are at once the most Known and the most Unknown about individual existence in this world.

4

SUBMISSIVE S-M

In S-M circles it has become almost cliché to say that "the submissive has all the power." In fact, as we continue to discover the secrets of Carnal Alchemy, we find out that we need to modify this statement somewhat. Submissives do not really "have" the power: they are the power. In the most polarized sense, the submissive incarnates or crystallizes the power, and the dominant develops and wields the power to magical ends. As we shall see, however, submissives, too, can cause changes to occur according to their own wills, but they do so as the power, not with the power.

In today's society the complex world of social dynamics, especially as it relates to the relationship between the sexes, is in clear evidence. The potential magical power inherent in this complex social network hinges on the idea of an exchange of power and the increase of mutual power between individuals. A certain question of dominance and submission exists in the relationship between the sexes, or between any two individual humans at any moment in that relationship. One will dominate the other; one will be the master, the other the slave. It must be pointed out that there is a real kind of power to be gained in being the slave as well—it all depends on the nature of the master and what the slave gets in exchange for her (or his) slavery.

A kind of magic comes into play here through a definite psychological mechanism. Some elements of mankind need a certain amount of misery, pain, and slavery. This inherent need will inevitably be played out in life one way or another. Because most people are unconscious of this need in themselves it simply gets played out in unhappy circumstances of life. This becomes what might be called "self-destructive masochism." Actual misfortune and misery are the only result. But if one is a "self-affirming masochist," who is conscious of this element in the personality, and who lives it out in a creative and self-aware manner, then the actual misery can be "exorcised" in a pleasurable and fun way.

In Carnal Alchemy the dominant takes the role of the alchemist, while the submissive is the very substance being transformed: to begin with perhaps "lead," but at the end of the process the purest "gold." Magically speaking the working of submissive Carnal Alchemy is most effective when you are trying to change things about yourself—in other words the subjective universe.

In the first chapter we pointed out that greater magic can work either on the outer world, or on the inner world of the magician. Due to the "mechanics" of the role of the submissive in Carnal Alchemy, this role is found to be most directly effective in work on the inner world of the submissives themselves—although we shall see how this can be turned back onto the objective outer world as well.

In general it seems best if Sado-Magicians can begin their involvement as submissives. The reasons for this are manifold. You cannot teach that which you yourself have not learned. On a very personal level it would be hard for dominants to command any respect from their submissives if it is known that they had never suffered the torments and humiliations they were now inflicting on their submissives. It seems fundamentally wrong, or unfair.

Beyond this respect issue is the fundamental principle of knowledge. If dominants don't know how a particular technique feels, how can they be expected to use it effectively? They will not have the necessary level of empathy to wield the whip or cane with the right amount of force and placement. They may err by being too severe, but it is more likely that they will make the mistake of being too merciful. For transformation to take place pain thresholds must be pushed and expanded. If someone does not know what crossing these thresholds feels like "from the inside" under the guidance of a knowledgeable dominant, it is unlikely that he or she will truly understand the process and thus will not be able to do the things necessary to facilitate the kind of transformative experiences we are talking about.

An additional reason it is best to start out as a submissive is one of pure enjoyment. How much pleasure can dominants derive from the Sadean experience if they don't even know what it feels like to be bound, spanked, or humiliated in an erotic context? They will only have recourse to their imaginations—uninformed by real fleshly experience. In such an instance the wannabe dominant might just as well watch some S-M videos and not even deal with real people. But if you have carnal knowledge of the feelings—tactile and emotional—that the submissive is experiencing, your experience will be multiplied and deepened.

For Carnal Alchemy to work there must be a high degree of precise understanding on the part of the dominant and a high level of passion and desire on the part of the submissive. In order to be a good dominant you have to be thinking and using your mental as well as sensual faculties much of the time. To be a good submissive, however, you have to maintain a certain balanced state of mind, heart, and body, which allows you to submit to pain and restriction, to the humiliation and discipline. Submissives are only responsible for themselves and their own internal reactions to what is happening to them. By contrast, dominants are usually responsible for everything from the configuration of the session to the correct sequencing and execution of each technique. It is also of the utmost importance to watch every reaction of submissives and to read them carefully to know how to proceed.

If all this has seemed too theoretical, let's take an everyday example of how Carnal Alchemy can work for an individual. We are reminded of the situation of a young man named Jeremy. Nothing in Jeremy's life seemed to go right. He had difficulty in the workplace, in maintaining relationships; and minor things always seemed to be going wrong. Jeremy was obviously an unwitting victim of unconscious masochism. An astute observer of modern life has observed that everybody needs some "suffering" in their lives—it seems to be a part of the human condition. Some need more than others. If you are unconscious of this need, Nature will simply deal out your lot of suffering in the most opportunistic ways—as She did with Jeremy. But one day Jeremy decided to fulfill a long-standing fantasy of his and answered a notice by an O∴ T∴ Dominatrix in a local alternative newspaper. She began a curriculum of severe training for him. After a number of these Sadean experiences, Jeremy noticed that his life seemed to be improving. Things that used to go "wrong" now went "right"—that is, more according to his conscious will. The reason for this is that now what used to be unconscious was made conscious. Instead of allowing Nature to be his Mistress, he chose his own Mistress. Instead of his "suffering" being dealt out blindly, it was received willingly—and even pleasurably.

In terms of Carnal Alchemy, the submissive corresponds to the very substance that is being transformed by the alchemical process. Submissive Sado-Magicians may start out in this process as something akin to "lead," but when the process is complete, they have become pure gold. This substance is a complex mixture of the physical, emotional, cognitive, and spiritual elements present in the submissive's personal makeup—it is the total

Being of that person. Ideally the process ends with these elements integrated and empowered.

The "Work" of the submissive is focused in the sexual and emotional centers. It is here that the attention of the submissive should be allowed to rest. If the submissive is somehow made to worry about the "details" of the rite, this focus can be lost to the detriment of the whole process.

As mentioned above the main area of focus of submissive Work in Carnal Alchemy is upon the subjective universe, that is, upon inner self-transformation. In this process the inner Being of every Substance of the submissive is broken down and recombined in higher forms of existence. Examples of aims of this kind of Work range from the psychomotor realm, where unwanted physical habits can be eliminated, to the emotive realm, where self-esteem can be enhanced and developed, to the cognitive realm, where all sorts of mental and reflective faculties can be crystallized. Submissives can be "trained" to stop biting their nails, to feel like a God or Goddess, to hone intellectual skills—and most importantly to develop spiritual awareness. This is not done as outsiders might expect through a system of rewards and punishments the way you might train an animal. Such an approach is contrary to the very essence of Carnal Alchemy. Rather it is a matter of changing the core Being in chemical and symbolic ways, according to magical archetypes. Any new behaviors then result not from outer changes but from essential inner transformations.

Magically submissive Sado-Shamans project onto the physical, emotional, and sexual images of the dominants the ideal qualities or characteristics by which they wish to be transformed. As a quasi-divine figure, the dominant will only be able to create something that is in his or her own "image." The same thing can also be said of all true artists—who can only do (or create) that which is within them. Thus the dominant actually becomes the Transformator or Transformatrix of the submissive. The Transformator/trix is someone consciously chosen by the submissive, and thus the transformational process ideally becomes a manifestation of the true will of the submissive as well as the dominant.

Beyond the persona of the dominant, the very sequence of events in the session—the symbols used or evoked—are experienced and thus absorbed into the being of the submissive in the quest of the heart and sexuality to be transformed.

As a practical matter it has been noted that there is usually a difference between submissive men and women in how they relate, or want to relate, to their dominants. Men, it seems, are usually more comfortable being submissive to just about any woman, just because she is female. This is perhaps because men symbolically project onto their dominant the image of "the Goddess" more easily than women do with men. For women it seems more important not to submit to just any man as a symbol of "masculinity" or "the God," but to a particular man as a true manifestation of what it is they desire to submit to. Ideally, the dominant should be a true incarnation of the Master or Mistress—the God or Goddess.

Ultimately, at advanced stages of development the submissive can also make magical changes in the objective universe or outer world. This is done by means of the hidden bond that exists between the inner and outer worlds. If the changes made in the inner world are profound enough, and the magician wills it, these changes can be made to be reflected in the outer world as well. It is actually somewhat easier to make changes in the objective universe through submissive Carnal Alchemy than it is to make subjective changes through dominant activity, although both of these reversals of operative polarity are commonly practiced and can be effective.

In conclusion, we would like to point out that sometimes the submissive can engineer an entire session or ritual to great effect. This is especially to be advised if the submissive is substantially more advanced in Sado-Magic than the person assuming the dominant role, and if the nature of the ritual is experimental or pragmatic in nature. In such instances the submissive can prescribe the techniques and the sequence of techniques with the stipulation that the person assuming the dominant role will carry them out to the letter with no possibility of alteration. In such a scenario both the dominant and the submissive can more easily relax into their roles and let the process take its inevitable course . . .

5

DOMINANT S-M

There is an intense feeling of power that rises in the soul of dominants at that moment when submissives willingly lie utterly vulnerable to their cruelties. To have another put that much trust in you is in and of itself empowering, and the symbolic quality of having absolute power over another human being is something that can be used to great magical effect.

In Carnal Alchemy the dominant magician is the actual alchemist or magician who works upon the complex substance of the submissive and coordinates the magical effects and aims. If the submissive actually embodies the substance of the magical work and the power with which the magic works, the dominant is the magician, the artist, the creator.

When you are just starting out as a dominant it is perhaps ideal to have as your submissive someone who is experienced, and who has high tolerances for pain. This gives latitude to make minor mistakes without having the psychological consequences be too dire. The flexibility of the submissive will allow him or her to balance from within those instances when you are too light or too heavy. Another desirable situation is one in which you can have a variety of submissives to work with. This can be the case if you become involved in a club or society for the practice of Sadean sexuality.

In the early stages of training as a dominant you should spend most of your efforts mastering physical techniques and the ability to forge an empathetic link between you and your partner. If these two fundamentals are solid, your continued development will be equally sound.

The role of the dominant is very much like that of the artist, and the creative pleasure felt by the dominant is very much akin to that felt by the artist working in his or her medium of choice. Here we are again reminded of the way in which the Italian Renaissance artist Michelangelo sought out pieces of marble he felt already contained the image he was looking for, and then, through the blows of his hammer and chisel he "liberated" the image from the stone. This is the feeling a good dominant should have when working with a submissive—that nothing is being forced, that everything is an act of liberation and transformation.

The true Sadean is a facilitator of the self-aware Masochist's experience. In the relationship between the Sadist and the Masochist there is a true exchange of power in which both give something and both gain something they inherently need. There is also the recognition that the roots of the true Sadean impulse lie not in hatred or anger, but in jealousy or envy. In a way the Masochist can be viewed as a projection of the Sadist's own inner—or "demonic"—self. The Sadist then proceeds to train, control, and even punish a symbol of his or her "demonic self" through the magical medium provided by the body and soul of the Masochist.

The Sadist is also the Artist. The insightful definition of Sadeanism offered by Gorer ("the pleasure felt from the observed modifications on the external world produced by the will of the observer") is equally true of the Artist or Magician. In the work of all of these types something is imagined in the subjective universe and from there it is caused to come into being in the objective universe.

As an alchemist the dominant must focus awareness in the cognitive or intellective center. Dominants can never "lose their heads." But emotional involvement is also crucial. The major use of the emotive center is in forging the empathetic link. Dominants should literally be able to "feel their way into" the self of their submissives. Without this link no magic can take place for the dominant—he or she will be just a prop in the magic of the submissive! In addition this link will be a great source of enjoyment and empowerment for the dominant, but only if the dominant understands what it is the submissive is feeling. Such understanding comes only through knowledge combined with actual personal experience in the flesh.

In using a particular instrument to inflict sweet suffering on your submissive, there come those moments in which you might sense that your self, the self of your submissive, and the essence of the instrument or technique begin to feel as if they all made up one great threefold wholeness. You, your submissive, and the whip become one. These moments are precious and should be sought out and encouraged.

Dominant Carnal Alchemists work their wills directly onto the objective universe through the symbolic medium of the submissive who has become a representative of the objective universe: the macrocosm. As we know the human body has long been used as a magical symbol of the world, of the greater universe. In Indo-European mythology the world order is said to have been shaped from the parts of the original cosmic man who was dissected and recombined (solve et coagula) by the great Gods of consciousness and magic to create a more perfect order.

In this there lies a great Mystery. If, through the use of the magical imagination and will, the symbolic link has been made strong between the essence of the submissive and that of the objective universe, alterations made in the experience and sensations of the submissive must inevitably reverberate in phenomena within the objective universe.

In a more complex way, dominant Sado-Magicians can also

work upon their own subjective universes by projecting that part of their inner selves they wish to transform onto the image of the submissive and then by making the right adjustments in that image by training it to do your will. By magical empathetic linkage the outer alteration inevitably will be reflected in the soul of the active partner. In this way the submissive becomes a living magical substance, with empathetic links to the being of the dominant. Working with a living body has more potential for power than working with inert images.

This is the essence of the alchemical experience. The alchemists of the Middle Ages manipulated various natural elements in the vegetable and mineral kingdoms, analogically identifying themselves and their own spiritual development with the manipulations they were carrying out. As they transmuted lead into gold, so too were their own base characteristics transformed into noble ones. As magical smiths forged perfect swords, so too were they perfecting themselves. The Carnal Alchemist, or Sado-Magician, has just taken this process to its most radical extreme—why work in the relatively inert masses of minerals and vegetables when the semidivine medium of an actual human being is available? For these techniques to be at all effective, the submissive must always be a part of the work in a completely willing way. If it's not consensual, it's not Carnal Alchemy or Sado-Magic.

It has long been recognized that often dominants, when they are torturing their submissives, are "really torturing themselves." Or at least the good ones will be able to have this feeling. This reminds us of some lines from a poem by the French poet Charles Baudelaire, the title of which is "Heauton Timoroumenos": Greek for "the Self-Tormentor."

I am the knife and the wound it deals,
I am the slap and the cheek,
I am the wheel and the broken limbs,
hangman and victim both!

I am the vampire at my own veins,
one of the great lost horde
doomed for the rest of time, and beyond,
"to laugh—but smile no more."*

Dominants must fulfill many roles. They may be part teacher, part actor, part caretaker, part taskmaster—and all magician. The ability to "put on a good show"—to mystify and amaze the submissive, to bring him or her into the alternate universe, which you have created—is no small accomplishment. Attention to detail must be great. Dominants are to create total experiences for their submissives, taking all of their senses and aspects of their beings into account.

A special word must be said about the role of the dominant as a caretaker. As a dominant you are responsible for the safety and experience of the submissive who has consented to put his or her body, heart, and psyche under your control. Submissives should always be given a "safe-word," which, if they speak it, means you are obligated to stop whatever it is you are doing immediately. Another word might be given, which, if uttered, can end the session altogether. If the relationship between the dominant and submissive is strong and the empathetic link well developed, the submissive should never have to use this "safe-word." Some also use "back-off" words, which indicate to the dominant that the

---

*This last line is quoted from Edgar Allen Poe's poem "The Haunted Palace."

discomfort is getting close to being unbearable, and they need a break. In the Triskelion this is thought to let the dominants off too easy. They should be in empathetic link well enough so that the "back-off" word becomes unnecessary. Also the internal tension in the submissive to hold out and overcome the pain thresholds is stronger if no "back-off" word is possible. The "back-off" option is most valuable in more playful situations.

There is no magical or emotional experience that quite compares to that of using the body of another (or your own body) as the ultimate symbol of the magical universe. While others may use cups and daggers for symbolic plays, the Carnal Alchemist goes to the ultimate source of power—physically, emotionally, as well as psychically—and works in the most radical way possible for human beings to work.

6

HOW TO WORK

Now the time for history and theory is past. Now it is time to put what we know into practice. Practice can begin in modest ways at first. Because S-M sexuality is customarily highly ritualized, according to the tastes of those involved, there is often no need for elaborate additional ritual. But such ritual can be enhancing to pleasure in its own right if it is not allowed to become a job.

The word "Work" may seem out of place in the title of this chapter. "Play" might have been more expected—in the sense of the Lila of the tantric Gods and Goddesses. But true Work, that is something you do for yourself, not others, should be virtually identical to that sort of Play. Sado-Shamanism, although a serious spiritual undertaking, should always be imbued with a spirit of erotic pleasure and enjoyment—*Lila*. This type of spiritual and magical Work is engaged in not because the participants are forced to do it by tradition or circumstance but because they desire to engage in it.

OPERATIVE PERSONAE

S-M sexuality often involves the participants playing roles. In the realm of traditional magical practice this is carried to the next level with so-called "assumption of god-forms." In tantrism the male and female partners are thought to embody the God and Goddess respectively in their acts of sexual worship. Thus the use of these ideas in Carnal Alchemy is really only a natural extension of what is practiced both in what might be called conventional S-M play and traditional magical practice. These roles, or personae, are tools for the practical exercise of the aims of Carnal Alchemy.

The Greek word *persona* originally meant a "mask." This was the kind of mask worn by the actors in ancient Greek dramas.

Masks have also been a part of conventional S-M play for over two hundred years. These masks may be used as actual physical pieces of equipment either by the Dominant (to enhance a certain kind of role being embodied) or by the Submissive (generally to obliterate the individual personality). Or we may refer to the masks as something symbolic of various roles being played by participants in an S-M ritual.

It is virtually stereotypical of S-M sexuality that certain roles are played by the participants: the schoolmaster and the naughty schoolgirl, the barbaric queen and her slave-boy, et cetera ad infinitum. Combined with the principles of Carnal Alchemy this "role-playing game" aspect of S-M conventions can be turned into a powerful ritual tool. As some types of literature are driven by "plot," while others might have the plot generated from the nature of the characters, so, too, can a Working of Sado-Magic be driven as much by the personae, or masks, assumed rather than the mechanics of any set ritual.

It is important to have a repertoire of personae with which you are comfortable and that your partners will feel are stimulating and practical for the purposes you are practicing Carnal Alchemy. Such personae are used by both the dominant and submissive practitioners.

There is a remarkably wide range of dominant personae available to Carnal Alchemists: For males, examples of these might be the no-nonsense husband or lover, the strict father, the schoolmaster, or the cruel sexual taskmaster, just to name a few. More apparently magical personae such as the sovereign god or cruel pagan priest might also be imagined, but the roles need not be overtly "magical" in the conventional sense to be effective operatively. For females a similar list might include the governess, the slave mistress, the wicked aunt, or prison matron—the list could go on and on. The key to the discovery of a naturally symbolic dominant persona is that the persona represented by the role should be one that naturally and quite plausibly holds power over others, either in some historical epoch of the past or in present times.

Suitable dominant personae can actually be discovered. You should conduct a number of sessions of imaginative exercise to discover the spectrum of personae you can work with as a dominant. First make a list of the types of personae you have imagined yourself being in a sexual fantasy context, and then expand the list by imagining other kinds of dominant personae. The list should be considered for the practical applications of the personae for Sado-Magic. From a pragmatic standpoint the personae you will use must 1) be sexually stimulating to you and your partner and 2) convey the kind of power you wish exercised in the Working of Carnal Alchemy. At the same time you should conduct a mirroring set of exercises to discover the kinds of submissive personae that you find most interesting and stimulating for your submissive partner to assume.

In theory you are to become this persona both for the sake of your own internal effectiveness as well as for the sake of providing the proper magical stimulus to the psyche of your partner. You should become this persona for the duration of the Working. Here the techniques used by actors to generate a total persona from within are most beneficial. The creation of a myth or background story for the persona might help in generating this internal quality. Besides working from within, you can also work from without in the shaping of the operative persona by correct costuming or the donning of certain symbolic articles of clothing or gear that will help you make the transformation from your mundane persona to the operative or magical one.

The development of submissive personae are not less important than the dominant ones. However, it is found that the submissive persona is often much more subtle and internal than the dominant ones. This is only natural as the operative work of a submissive is more introverted, while that of the dominant is by nature more extroverted.

The spectrum of submissive personae available to Carnal Alchemists is a reflection of the dominant personae: For males typical submissive personae include the well-disciplined husband or lover, the obedient nephew, the schoolboy, or the sexual slave of a cruel mistress, just to name a few. For females a similar list might include the domestically disciplined wife or lover, the slavegirl, the contrite schoolgirl, or female prisoner—again this is just a partial list to jog some thoughts. The key to the discovery of naturally symbolic submissive personae is that the personae represented need to be ones that are naturally given to being under the power or control of another person—and again this can be inspired by historical imagery as well as contemporary situations.

Submissive personae can also be discovered. Carry out a similar set of exercises in imagination as might be conducted for the discovery of dominant personae. Initially a list of the types of personae you have imagined yourself being in some sexual fantasy—then extend that list according to the principles outlined above. Pragmatic considerations must always be kept at the forefront: the personae you use must be both sexually exciting to you and your partner, and they must embody the type of power you wish to express in your Working of Sado-Magic. As a part of this exercise also, you will discover the kinds of dominant personae you might wish your partner to assume.

Again the theory is that you should first become the kind of submissive persona that you find appealing to assume for yourself and one that is stimulating for your partner as well. Techniques for generating this persona again would include the development of a mythic background story. Historically either rituals of all kinds were illustrations of mythic material or the myths were developed from the ritual practices. In any event, ritual and meta-narrative or myth go hand in hand. Once more, certain articles of costuming or gear will help reinforce this metamorphosis of personae. So often the placement of a collar and/or ankle and wrist cuffs on a slave will act as a psychic trigger to place the submissive into his or her persona.

In the practice of operative personae it is always of the utmost importance to remember to keep things pragmatic. By that we mean focus on things that help stimulate a sexual response, for that sexual excitement is the great reservoir of power you will draw from in any act of Carnal Alchemy or Sado-Magic. Those who practice sexual magic and assume exotic Eastern god-forms because a book has told them this is how Indian tantrics do it should not wonder then why the magic doesn't seem to work as well as it should. Unless you are especially turned on sexually by exotic Asian costumes and accoutrements, then such trappings are unnecessary. What works for you sexually is the key to what will work for you magically because the idea is to build up the energy to the highest levels possible so that this energy can be directed as you will it.

THE RITUAL

The basic format of the simplest Working consists of four parts:

1. Plan the session
2. Enter the chamber
3. Conduct the session
4. Exit the chamber

Many experienced dominants might remark at this point: "That's what I do for ordinary sessions!" Indeed, that is because performances of even what appears to be "non-spiritual," or "non-magical" Sado-Masochistic sessions are usually highly ritualistic and symbolic, with scenarios that are driven by the archetypal character of the personae being assumed.

Plan the Session

Transformational rites or so-called rites of passage have long been recognized in anthropological circles. Universally these consist of three parts: rites of separation, rites of transformation, and rites of reinclusion. In these rites personas are transformed from one state of being to another. Candidates for initiation are first formally separated from their "normal" environment, then in that special set-apart place they are metamorphosed by sometimes complex experiential rituals, and then finally reintegrated back into their normal environment as a transformed individual.

From a truly magical perspective, the most experienced and accomplished Sado-Magicians will find that the most important phase of the ritual really takes place before anyone ever enters the chamber. In planning the session with magical and/or spiritual intent the events of the actual physical session will be automatically "charged" with the levels of significance and meaning intended or willed by the planner. (This is true whether from the dominant or the submissive perspective.)

In thinking out the ritual/session the symbolic meaning of all the actions should be made conscious—each aspect of the session should be planned with an understanding of the meaning of that aspect. Of course, all of these things must also be planned out within the parameters of the submissive's tolerances and desires as well. The session/ritual should be composed and written out just as one might compose or structure any ceremony. You may or may not refer to the written document during the actual session—and you may deviate from it based on inspiration or on alterations made necessary because of modifications in the submissive's state of being—you may find that you have to back off on some things you were going to try, or you may find that you will be able to go further in some areas. The reasons the plan needs to be written out are 1) to make a magical record of your experiment (all magicians and alchemists should keep records of their Workings and experiments) and 2) the act of objectifying the plan on paper has the effect of making the plan objectively real and hence more effective. Also it is easier to remember the sequence of things if they have been previously objectified in this way.

But remember the plan is always just a hypothesis, which can be altered at any time to suit the situation at hand. In Carnal Alchemy, until such hypothesized rituals are proven to work between two people, they do not become sacred practice.

Once the symbolic meanings of the planned actions have been made conscious, they can begin to be "forgotten" or allowed to slip back down below the threshold of consciousness so they can work on deeper unconscious magical levels.

During the actual session it is generally not necessary to dwell on the magical or spiritual meaning of the actions—those have already been established. Your chief task inside the chamber is to fulfill the vision of the ritual or session in the most powerful way possible. Let go and let the magical aspect work for you as an inner guide, to not allow yourself to be consciously involved in the mechanics once the session has begun.

Among other important aspects of preparation for the session are the physical arrangements. These are three in number: 1) The chamber must be organized and fitted with everything needed to carry out the session. This is usually done by the dominant, of course. 2) The dominant must also prepare mentally and emotionally—dressing for the mood being evoked may be essential in this regard. 3) The submissive must also prepare—here preparation of the body and the emotions is essential.

Enter the Chamber

At the appointed time the participants enter the chamber (however they conceive of it)—and the profane world is left behind until they reemerge. Upon entering the chamber, the everyday world is forgotten and a special "alternate universe" is entered. In this universe wishes come true and fantasies become reality. If you do not have a special room set aside for a chamber, the "chamber effect" can be achieved through a number of symbolic ways: hang a certain evocative picture or image on the wall, cover the mundane furniture in the room, light symbolic candles, and so on. The chamber itself is discussed in detail in chapter 8.

The important thing is that you create the effect of entering your own private "alternate universe" for the duration of the session. It has also been found to be effective to rent a hotel room for session activities, which also can give an "exotic" feel.

Conduct the Session

Carnal Alchemy is and must be a highly pragmatic form of sexual magic. The imperatives for a successful ritual of Sado-Magic have their origins in what would make a successful session of Sadean sexuality even if magic were not overtly involved. If the S-M aspect of the session does not work, it is unlikely that the magical aspect will. This is why the partners involved in a Working of Sado-Magic should already know what works for them erotically before trying to undertake an act of Carnal Alchemy.

An effective structure for a session has been found to include several phases. The initial phase usually orients submissives in their role and helps them start to get into their own bodies and experiences. One effective way to do this is through a ceremony in which submissives are fitted with their collars and cuffs—as symbols of their roles—and ordered to recite any rules that have been given to them. They may also be formally asked if they are indeed there of their own free will, for it is magically essential that this be so. Such ceremonies (also common in "non-magical" Sado-Masochism) anchor submissives in their emotional feelings (with the rules and verbal exchanges).

Subsequent phases are planned so as to increase the intensity of stimulation the submissive is to suffer—whether it is physical or emotional. Common sense dictates that if your submissive has never been caned, that you would not start off with the cane, for example. More severe methods must be built up to slowly—this ensures the highest possible tolerances. Again, this book is not intended as a book on general Sadean methods—which must be learned before a tremendous amount of success can be expected in Carnal Alchemy.

Experience will show you how Sadean sexuality is not oriented toward the orgasm. In Sadean sessions orgasms often seem "anticlimactic." The slow, yet steady and powerful, release of sexual energy throughout the session is often far more satisfying and fulfilling than any orgasm. This is especially so for the dominant. This is because so much of the sexual or erotic energy is constantly being transmuted throughout the session that it may indeed feel like an orgasm that goes on for hours. Because the dominant is so strongly polarized between sexual desire and mental/spiritual creativity—by virtue of the very nature of the activity—the conduit between the physical/sexual center and the intellectual/spiritual center becomes wide open in ways that are difficult to obtain otherwise.

Sexual energies can be so totally sublimated or transmuted to the creative faculty that orgasm is not desired—this is the mark of a truly successful session or ritual from the perspective of the dominant. It is usually advisable to have the submissive achieve orgasm by whatever means seem right. The reasons for this are manifold: First, it gives a sense of "physical closure," which may be necessary for the submissive to get out of the persona assumed for the session. Also, the orgasm may be used by the dominant to "anchor" certain symbols or carnally alchemical reactions. This can be a major tool for transformation used by the dominant. Finally the orgasm is, after all, the elemental Fire of the alchemist—in it the transformations that have taken place in the session are crystallized and made solid. It is a great act of the recoagulating of the elements of the personality. If dominants also want to reintegrate elements of their personalities, closure of the session with orgasm is recommended. If orgasm is not achieved, the dominant may continue to walk around in a perpetually dynamized state, which can make one rather crazy after a while.

Exit the Chamber

Once the session activity has come to an end the participant may do one of two things: either remain in the chamber to "decompress" or leave the chamber immediately. In the first instance this is often the time when sexual activity of a more vanilla variety is engaged in between lovers as a way to "ground" themselves or to absorb into each other the transformations that have taken place. The immediate exit from the chamber is observed when the magic done in the chamber has been intended to have an effect on the outside world. In such an instance remaining in the chamber and "absorbing" the gathered energies would be counterproductive.

When the session/ritual is ended, depending on the intensity of emotion, sensation, and thought aroused, there is a period commonly called the "afterglow." The individuals involved in the session should enjoy this period in whatever way they feel will be most conducive to the intended results of the session. As a magical rule it is usually best to sever all conscious ties with the intention of the Working. Dwelling on the intention in a conscious way after the ritual is complete just tends to drain energy away, which would otherwise be on its way along unconscious streams to complete the will of the magicians. Exiting the chamber you sever physical links with the Work—this should be accompanied by an inner emotional and cognitive break with the aim of the Working as well. The work is done, it is in the past.

It will be noted that the "afterglow," although enjoyable for both dominant and submissive, is felt in very different ways by each. The submissive enjoys a feeling of a sort of natural "body high"—the result of the alterations in his or her psychopharmacology during the session combined with the strong emotional release felt in such instances. The dominant's "afterglow" is much more akin to the "high" actors get after a performance on stage. It is partly physical, but mostly emotional and intellectual—the elation at having successfully brought the whole thing off.

In the spirit of the idea of reinclusion, the time of the "afterglow" is perhaps best spent reintegrating the personalities involved into their normal or everyday states. It is a time to tend the sore muscles and welted flesh of the submissive—or in possibly more social situations, for all parties involved to come back to earth in a supportive and safe environment.

It should be noted that operative rites of the kind practiced by the Order of the Triskelion generally are never printed in a public forum. Printing and publishing such Workings would profane them and lead to manifold misunderstandings among those who do not grasp the true nature of the Workings. Initiatory rites may be printed, although they are kept in secret. There is certainly an inherent power in the keeping of such secrets. In any event it has often been found that the best way to record such rites and Workings is in the form of apparently fictional accounts.

7

WORKING
TECHNIQUES

As we mentioned in the preface, these techniques should not be tried without learning something about them from a living person—if at all possible—unless you are already very experienced in S-M sexuality with your partner and you are just widening your repertoire. This book is not intended as a "training manual" for dominants, but rather a commentary from a magical perspective on various methods common in Sadean sexuality.

The number of separate techniques you can use in S-M sexuality is endless. This infinite variety has ensured that S-M is a sexuality in which there are a thousand virginities to be lost—and a thousand to be taken.

Perhaps this is one of the reasons for the apparent complexity of the techniques involved. However, it must be said that Carnal Alchemy can be readily worked by using the simple technique of a basic over-the-knee spanking if that is what works for the individual(s) involved. The complexity is a tool, but not a necessity.

This possibility of virtually infinite variety and novelty in the sexual life of individuals holds out the promise of great power when viewed from a magical angle. Also the fact that magic is a technology of hidden powers and S-M is a form of sexuality, which hinges on a very similar idea, makes them natural allies in the human quest to uncover the hidden avenues of life.

We must emphasize the absolute necessity for that empathetic link between the dominant and submissive. If this link or bond is present, almost any method can be used safely because the dominant is "in touch" with the feelings and reactions of the submissive, if it is not present, almost any technique can be dangerous. Also, although there are actually hundreds of methods to be mastered in a technical sense, if the magically forged empathetic bond has been formed by the dominants and are guided by that link in the application of every technique, they will be able to work successfully and safely with almost all techniques. Stay in touch with your submissive. This is necessary in recreational S-M, and it is doubly so in the practice of Carnal Alchemy.

To begin with there are six major types of techniques commonly used among Sadeans—any of which can be employed for Sado-Magical ends:

1. Bondage
2. Flagellation
3. Piercing
4. Penetration
5. Clamping
6. Temperature (heat/cold)

Combined with these six in one way or another is the seventh element of sexual stimulation, which holds them all together and gives them their transformative edge.

These basic techniques in no way exhaust the possibilities—which are indeed endless. But they form a basic repertoire by which the art of Sado-Magic can be practiced. To break things down into what are perhaps the most essential technical components, you must be able to use three basic stimuli: 1) quantum pain (the kind given in quanta [incremental], such as strokes of a whip or the quick insertion of a needle) 2) continuum pain (the kind which is continuous and long as the stimulus is applied, such as clamps or that which certain modes of bondage provide) and 3) sexual stimulation. In the right combination, applied with the complete knowledge of the individual subject's responses and tolerances, these three become a Carnal Trinity, giving access to the realm beyond Heaven and Hell, beyond Pleasure and Pain.

BONDAGE

The purpose of bondage in Sado-Magic is manifold. It may be used to control the physical movement of the submissive so that when techniques involving pain are applied the submissive will be less likely to alter his or her position, causing an uncontrolled stroke or application.

A note should be added from the beginning that it is in the area of bondage where the greatest physical dangers lie in the area of S-M. Often among the public "bondage" is viewed as "maybe okay." What otherwise unimaginative partners haven't tied each other up for sex? But S-M—whipping, clamps, and so on—is viewed as "dangerous" or "sick." In fact more injuries are likely to occur through accident or misapplication of technique when using the methods of bondage than when using more strict S-M techniques. There are true bondage "artists" who might spend hours tying up their submissives in intricate works of art made of flesh, rope, and chain. This form of bondage constitutes a special craft within the D/S subculture itself. But most of the real physical effects achieved by these art forms can be accomplished with little technical skill in a matter of seconds.

Basic forms of physical bondage can be achieved easily by using leather cuffs on the wrists and ankles with the possible addition of a collar around the neck. These objects, usually put on as a part of a ceremony within the ritual or session, in combination with snap hooks and short lengths of rope or chain, can then serve to bind the submissive in just about any possible position and do so in a quick and easy fashion. These are also discussed a bit more in chapter 8.

Submissives can be bound in place for punishments, or the bondage itself can be a form of training. Many submissives work well using great amounts of muscle tension that can be built up in forms of restraint where they are held virtually immobile. Seabrook's "Dervish Dangling" is an example of how such bondage techniques are useful in and of themselves in magical operations.

One word of added warning: No submissive should be left in the chamber unattended while in bondage.

Beyond physical forms of bondage, there are some modes of working that might be referred to as "psychological bondage." These are restrictions placed upon the behavior of the submissive by the dominant. These include various rules that might be given to submissives—that they must stand or walk in a certain way, must address the dominant in a certain manner, or they are not allowed to say certain things or to touch themselves without permission—and so on into infinity. These psychological restrictions placed on submissives as rules serve a special purpose of disciplining and focusing their minds on their status in the chamber. Given what was said in chapter 4 about the focus of the submissive's attention on the physical, sexual, and emotional centers, it is most important that rules be created that will facilitate this focus in the submissive. Because these restrictions in behavior are focusing mechanisms, they can be sources of great magical power.

FLAGELLATION

The most classic forms of quantum pain are provided by flagellation: spanking, paddling, strapping, whipping, and caning. These are listed in ascending order of difficulty to master.

The simplest kind of flagellation is the slap of an open palm on the bare bottom cheek—and it is amazing how much such a simple act can fire the imagination. In fact this (at least formerly popular) form of parental discipline can be quite painful—but is unlikely to cause harm or injury. In Sadean activity it is now used as a sort of "warm up" phase for more severe things—although there is also a dedicated following totally devoted to this one act. Traditionally spanking is done over the knee or lap of the spanker (either sitting on the side of a bed or on an armless chair), or the one receiving the spanking can be bent over a chair or kneel on a bed. In an equally traditional fashion the victim is never bound for a spanking. Submissives must hold their positions of their own wills—although kicking of the legs is sometimes unavoidable. A spanking can go on for a long time and is usually delivered with fast strokes of the palm of the hand. The pain of a spanking is allowed to build and build—until the submissive can bear no more. The process can be repeated often.

The most traditional type of institutionalized corporal punishment in the United States during this century was the paddle—usually made of wood. The paddle can be very effectively used in Sadean sessions to deliver "quanta" of pain. This instrument can be made of wood or leather and be either of the elongated rectangular shape (so popular in American fraternities and elsewhere) or of the more rounded "ping-pong" variety. Paddles are almost exclusively used on the buttocks of the submissive.

Leather straps can also be used for flagellation, of course. The simplest form of this would be provided by the belt—another favorite of "traditional discipline." More elaborate kinds of straps are also used (such as the *tawse* or "prison strap"). With spanking and paddling the dominant does not have to worry about "wrap-around"—that is, the unintentional wrapping of the ends of the instrument being used around the side of the body, buttocks, or legs of the submissive. This can result in uncontrolled and overly severe impacts of the instrument at the tips. Such technical difficulties must be foreseen and learned about firsthand. Dominants only want to deliver just the quanta of pain they intend to deliver—no more and no less. Straps can be used on the back, buttocks, and legs of the submissive.

Whips come in an almost infinite variety. Some are simple to use, such as the quirt or riding crop, while others are extremely difficult—the ultimate being the bullwhip. The best common source for good whips is the local equestrian shop—although there are many extremely fine whip-makers in the S-M or Leather community as well. (Some of these can be found in the Resources section of this book.) Depending on the type of whip, they can be used on any part of the body, from the back to the most tender and vulnerable areas. Whips can also be made to give an almost infinite variety of sensation, from a cutting bite that can break the skin to a light tingling kiss.

Of the basic types of flagellation mentioned here, caning is the most difficult of the methods to master. Its effects can be very severe on the flesh of the submissive. A cane can be made of (*kooboo*) rattan or bamboo, be from an eighth to a quarter of an inch in diameter, and usually be anywhere between twenty and thirty-two inches in length. Canelike instruments made of synthetic material have recently become popular due to the fact that they can be cleaned of any body fluids. The cane was the instrument of choice for corporal punishment in British and Continental schools and penal institutions during the nineteenth and early twentieth centuries. The submissive is traditionally bound, most preferably over a wooden "horse" for the application of the cane. This is one instrument that absolutely should not be tried without guidance.

From a Sadean perspective it is only important that you have a way of delivering pain to your submissive in quanta of sufficient intensity so that his or her body will begin to release endorphins. For this, flagellation is the most traditional, most reliable, and probably the safest method.

PIERCING

There is something powerful about the symbolism of yielding, supple flesh being pierced by hard, cold steel. The great Japanese writer, Yukio Mishima, wrote that he had his first orgasm when he first looked upon an image of St. Sebastian with the martyr's flesh pierced with arrows.

It must be said from the outset that piercing can be dangerous and should only be tried by experienced and knowledgeable people. Safe practice is a special concern when it comes to breaking the skin. Piercing is only to be done with sterile needles. These needles must always be the types that are made to pierce living flesh. Do not use sewing needles, pins, and so on! These are far too dull. In these times proper needles can be hard to find.

Some remote pharmacies carry them, but the most likely source nowadays might be veterinary supply or feed stores. Needles used for permanent piercings can also be used for temporary ones, of course. Areas of the body that can be pierced temporarily are basically those that are often permanently pierced—the nipples, labia, skin of the penis, and scrotum. Once the needles are inserted, weights can be hung from them, or line attached to them to give some tension to the area of pierced skin. Here we see a modern reflection of the shamanic rites of the Plains Indians mentioned in chapter 2.

Needles can be inserted into the flesh, creating a "human pincushion" effect. Such piercings can be made to be no more painful than a shot in the doctor's office—although slow insertions are substantially more painful than quick ones! Also piercing the skin just below the surface is, of course, considerably more painful than direct vertical entry. A safety warning here, however: consult with a doctor (some are sympathetic) or a textbook on anatomy and physiology to determine the areas of the body that can be safely pierced in this way. Nerve pathways can be damaged easily. The sciatic nerve, which runs down the center of each buttock and down the center of the back of each thigh, must be avoided at all costs. Damage to this nerve can lead to chronic pain and disability! As with all techniques, if you aren't sure how to do it—don't!

Most permanent piercings may seem more readily classified in the area of cosmetics than as a Sadean technique. However, as exemplified in *Story of O* such piercings (and even brandings) can serve symbolic purposes in the aesthetic life of the Sadean. To be true symbols they must be the result of piercings done without anesthetic, and done in a ritual setting. Popular areas of the anatomy to be pierced in this way include the nipples, labia, (*majora* and *minora*), and a wide variety of possible penile and scrotal piercings.

PENETRATION

Penetration of the bodily orifices—especially the vagina and anus—are acts usually considered a part of vanilla sex. However, such penetrations are extremely useful in a Sadean context. First of all it must be remembered that sexual excitement—the transformative Fire—is essential to the Working of Carnal Alchemy. This can be and usually is present in submissives without genital or anal contact. Yet such penetrations (often with a dildo or other artificial device) can facilitate such excitement. But the true Sadean use of such penetrations comes in when such penetrations are made painful, at least initially, due to the size or surface texture of the object being inserted, or made humiliating in some way. Submissives may be trained to take larger and larger objects into their orifices—each time stretching them a bit more, each time causing them to have to struggle with the pain of the insertion. Since, as a rule, for these penetrations to be successful the submissive has to "give in" to the experience—and literally "open up" to accept the violation of the dominant—this technique is powerful both symbolically and physically.

Penetrations can indeed evoke a sense of "violation" and extreme vulnerability in the submissive. For this reason such methods are especially valuable to use on male submissives because they are not penetrated in vanilla sex and may not have this sense otherwise.

Perhaps the ultimate experience in this type of penetration

is the act known as "fisting" in which a dominant will thrust an entire hand and often forearm into the vagina or rectum of a submissive. This is often a painful and dangerous technique and requires in-depth training for both persons.

CLAMPING

Under the general category of "clamping" we would place any technique that restricts the blood supply to or from various areas of the body. One of the basic ways to accomplish this is with rope, cord, line, rubber tubing, rubber bands, and so forth—applied to areas such as the female breasts or the male genitals. This method causes swelling in these erogenous zones but is rarely painful in and of itself. However, once the binding is complete, the areas in question are well presented and sensitized for further punishments.

More strictly speaking, clamps are devices used to pinch small areas of flesh. These can be light or quite severe. Such clamps may be obtained commercially, or a hardware or variety store can be an innovative source for such equipment. Everything from clothespins to alligator clips and battery clamps (available in a diabolical array in neighborhood electronic shops) can be used. These are most commonly applied to the nipples. A word of warning: Do not apply these devices right on the tip of the nipple—the "bite" of the clap should come just behind the nipple on the aureola. Clothespins can be applied all over the body—anywhere there is enough supple skin for them to hold.

As a rule, such clamps are more painful coming off than they are either going on or while they are in place. They should not be left on for very long. The dominant should check the circulation in the clamped area frequently. If the flesh becomes numb or cold and pale/blue, the clamps should be removed immediately.

Weights can also be hung from the clamps and clips of this kind. These will add to the tension and incrementally increase the pain. The use of clamps and weights is perhaps the best way of delivering continuous pain to your submissive in a controlled and safe way (as long as the submissive's neurovascular and circulatory status in the clamped area is checked frequently).

TEMPERATURE

The application of heat to the skin of the submissive can be a powerful symbolic act as well as being a dramatic kind of pain. The most common mode of delivering heat to the skin comes in the form of hot wax. The easiest and safest way to do this is by dripping wax from a lit candle onto the skin surface. The further away the candle is from the skin the cooler the wax will be when it hits the skin's surface. To increase the heat and the intensity of the sensation just bring the candle closer to skin. Candles made of softer wax melt at lower temperatures, and wax from them is therefore not as hot. So-called "dripless" candles (which can be made to drip) are not recommended, and beeswax candles are to be avoided as their wax can actually burn the skin.

In general the use of candle wax is safe and can be quite effective. The only drawback is that it tends to make a mess and be unaesthetic after the waxing is done.

A more advanced technique, not to be tried by beginners, is the use of hot needles, or as we romantically refer to it, "Devil Fire." Ideal for this technique are those needles used for dissection purposes in biology labs. They are available in scientific supply stores. Suitable and perhaps more aesthetic versions can also be fashioned from sewing needles (at least two inches long) set in the ends of wooden dowels. These are to be heated and then applied to the skin. At first only the points of them should be lightly touched on the surface of the flesh. Then at more advanced stages the hot metal can be laid lengthwise on the skin. If the needles are heated to high temperatures the burns caused by them will leave scars that will last from a few weeks to many months. Do not heat the needles in candle flames. Use only a clean burning flame. This is most easily obtained from the use of jelly fuels, of the kind used for camping or fondue pots.

The application of objects that are very cold to the skin of a submissive can often have effects very similar to those of heat. Ice cubes or metal objects (such as chains, needles, and so on that have been frozen in a freezer) will do for this technique. Interesting physical effects may be generated by oscillating between hot and cold objects.

A sensation very close to that of heat and cold is often created by various mentholated ointments, tiger balsam, peppermint oil, powdered ginger, and so on. These are applied directly to the skin; only those substances that are safe to ingest orally should be placed in or around the mucous membranes of the urethra, vulva, or anus. Many "sports rubs" with ingredients such as methyl salicylate should never be used in those areas.

Other major areas of interest often explored by Sado-Magicians and Shamans might include enemas, sensory deprivation, electricity, asphyxiation, catheterization, cutting/scarification, branding, suspension, golden showers, corseting, "forced" cross-dressing, tickling, abrasion, public humiliation . . .

The reason any technique is used is always twofold. First, it can be simply arousing or exciting to the people involved—thus it can help fulfill the requirement in sexual magic that excitement be raised to the highest levels—regardless of methods. But on the other level, on the more particularly Sado-Magical level, methods are to be applied that are difficult for the one suffering them to bear. Barriers must be broken; thresholds of pain and pleasure must be crossed, violated, and transformed. In this there can arise a problem. With regard to the use of painful stimuli in magic a German expert on sexual magic, Frater U∴ D∴, has stated

> Physical pain tends to dull the senses in the long run, so that stimuli have to be increased incessantly. This may quite easily lead to grave bodily harm, not to mention the fact that it can become downright addictive and lead to a kindled frenzy not very easily mastered. Furthermore, such practices usually involve a great deal of paraphernalia, precise dramatizing, and plenty of physical and psychological energy . . .[1]

These words are very true. Lucretius, an epicurean Roman philosopher of the first century BCE, pointed out that pleasure, not pain, is the natural state of the body. The body is equipped with natural chemical mechanisms for alleviating pain, and humans only have a limited capacity to suffer pain until it is either turned to pleasure or is anesthetized through numbness. Our capacity for pleasure, however, can be made infinite. Since all of this is true, special practices must be observed to ensure that thresholds of endurance remain at manageable levels.

This is accomplished in two ways. First, within a session, you can vary your methods. Don't keep using flagellation until the pain tolerances have built up so high that you have to use a

Russian knout to get the physiological results you desire. Use flagellation until high tolerance is reached, then switch to another technique—the application of heat or clamps, for example. Later you can return to a flagellation technique with renewed effects.

For most people you will find that although their Sado-Magical tolerances for one type of pain may be high, they are no more than average with another. Even within a given technique this may be true. Some may adore the sensation of the cane but find that of the leather strap almost unbearable.

The second way to manage thresholds of endurance over a longer time span is to refrain from engaging in S-M activities at all for a while. If you are lucky enough to be in a relationship with someone who can be both dominant and submissive, you may consider a periodic switch of roles in order to manage this potential problem.

Here we have purposefully not discussed psychological techniques. As delicate as the physical techniques are to master effectively, the psychological ones make them pale by comparison. By "psychological techniques" we mean everything from the personas the dominant might assume and the ones they demand of their submissives to the verbal symbolism used in the chamber.

It is perhaps in this area of psychological methodology where the greatest number of mistakes is made. A misplaced whip-stroke is much less harmful in any lasting way than a misplaced word or symbol. The best way to avoid these problems and at the same time take advantage of the power provided through the use of such psychological techniques is to communicate extensively with your partner outside the chamber. Find out what words, phrases, gestures, and so forth, excite arousal, shame, humiliation. . . . Then discover whether these feelings are, in fact, detrimental to the experience of the submissive. Once these things are discovered, the dominant can act accordingly.

The communication necessary for this level of activity is assured through the proper use of the "Triskelion Process" or "Triskelion Game." Find out what excites your partner and what his or her fantasies are. Then you will have a much better idea as to whether he or she wants to be shamed or humiliated, and if so, how.

8

THE CHAMBER

THE CHAMBER AND EQUIPAGE

Activity as sacred as Carnal Alchemy or Sado-Magic is often thought to deserve a special place in the home or apartment set aside for it alone. Having a chamber, or "dungeon," just for this part of one's life has a special purpose as well. It is usually the case that partners do not live out the dominant/submissive lifestyle twenty-four hours a day, seven days a week—and in such cases it is valuable to have a space set aside that symbolizes that part of their lives together. It is also true that entering such a space can trigger certain responses in the souls of the participants, which allow them greater psychological freedom—both from within themselves and with regard to their partners—to live out their innermost fantasies to the fullest.

Such a chamber can also be a place where the artistry and imagination of the participants can be expressed—not only in the activity there but also in the actual design and equipping of the room. And since it is unlikely that you will be offered a videotape deal on cable TV telling you how to outfit your home dungeon, we will just have to provide some basic help in this chapter. Also take advantage of the material offered in the resources section at the end of this book.

A word of warning though: all the fancy equipment in the world won't make your magical and erotic adventures something they wouldn't otherwise be. The equipment can only enhance what is already there. If the spirit and empathy are not right, no amount of furniture or "infernal contraptions" will help. But because these arts are so involved with a fairly complex set of aesthetic rules and ceremonies, and because there is often the need to be able to move smoothly through a wide variety of physical sensations, the equipping of at least a minimally furnished chamber is highly recommended.

PURPOSE OF THE CHAMBER

The initial purpose of the chamber or dungeon is to set your activities apart from the rest of your life. This is not a means to "protect" your everyday life from the results of your Sadean practices—for we know the effects of such scenarios are almost universally beneficial—but rather the intention is to intensify the feelings and energies generated by such activity. The chamber functions in a way similar to that of the laboratory for scientists or the studio for artists or the temple for magicians. It contains and focuses the activities that they may be more pure, more intense, and more powerful.

If you go back to our discussion of how transformations are made you will see that there must be an act of separation, of isolation of the subjects from outside influences: this must take place before the transformational play is enacted. It is after this that the subjects are reintegrated, reincluded, into the mundane world. The chamber is meant to enhance this process and this experience.

The "chamber effect" can be obtained in several ways. You can, of course, have a special room set aside to serve exclusively as a "playroom," or you can make some modifications to a room being used for some other purpose that can be converted quickly and easily into such a room. A cellar, garage, or attic space is ideally suited for the "multiple-purpose room." Many will find it necessary to make their own master bedroom into the chamber. In such an event the importance of certain symbolic or ceremonial actions and/or objects becomes relatively more important.

When a room normally used for more "mundane" purposes is to be temporarily transformed into a Sadean chamber, don't forget to take some time to figure out how to transform the entire atmosphere of the room into something special. Fabrics can be used to drape over furniture; pictures or other decorations not conducive to the atmosphere should be removed or draped. Candles or perhaps red and/or blue lightbulbs can be used for illumination. (Such dim lighting may be hazardous for inexperienced dominants who must often gauge the severity of some of their activities by alterations in the skin tone of their submissives, since especially red light makes red marks on the skin virtually invisible!)

As we have said elsewhere, the dominant and the submissive should perhaps both have certain symbolic signs of their relative positions that they put on, or have put on them, at some point before or at the very beginning of a session. Often this is a collar and/or cuffs for the slave and perhaps certain articles of clothing for the master/mistress. The particular aesthetic choice is, of course, entirely up to the persons involved. However, the point of bringing this subject up here is to emphasize this act as an act of separation—of creating of the "chamber effect."

The use of symbols—especially highly discreet ones such as finger rings—can be very useful in creating "chambers beyond chambers" when sessions are to be enacted outside the playroom or over extended periods of several hours or even days. This is the importance of the triskelion signet ring given to O before she leaves Roissy for the first time. In reality she did not leave Roissy—for through the ring it surrounds her always.

DESIGN OF THE CHAMBER

Any well-equipped chamber should have the means for positioning (and restraining, if necessary) the submissive in at least three basic postures: standing, lying, and bending (over an easy chair, horse, etc.). It will also, by whatever means, have, or be capable of taking on, a very special atmosphere. This atmosphere is gained through a combination of interior design principles (furniture, wall hangings, wall color, etc.) and other sensory tools such as mirrors, music, lighting, even incense and special drinks. All the senses are to be considered—to enhance them, subject them to pain or pleasure, or to deprive them.

Certain pieces of equipment are best built into the structure of the chamber or room. There should be a way to fix the submissive in a horizontal or lying position (a bed or bedlike rack is ideal for this), and a way to fix him or her in a standing position.

The vertical position can also easily be achieved with a minimum of alteration to the room by anchoring a large eyebolt into a brace in the ceiling. This should be secured and tested to be sure that it could bear the entire weight of the person who is to be secured to it. This should not, however, be used for actual suspension of the person's full weight. Suspension has special requirements and should not be tried by beginners. Also you should consider using "panic" snap hooks, which make it easy for submissives to release themselves and allow dominants to release submissives very quickly in case of an emergency.

The easiest way to create a horizontal surface is, of course, to modify an existing bed. Four-posters are ideal for this. Eyebolts may be added to the posts, or leather straps looped around them (to which perhaps short lengths of chain have been attached) to allow for tying the submissive in a spread-eagle position. Such chain-straps are also useful for fixing submissives either in or over chairs and other pieces of furniture.

The bending position can be achieved with sofas, chairs, or with the "horse" especially designed for this purpose, which is discussed below.

There should also be a way to store and/or display the various sorts of equipment used in your activities. It is not very masterful, or conducive to concentration, to have to rummage around in a pile of whips and chains to find just the right one at just the right moment.

Although a knowledgeable Master or Mistress can create a minimally effective chamber in a matter of minutes in a hotel room or any living room, bedroom, or den, it is also aesthetically pleasing to have special pieces of furniture created for specific Sadean purposes.

BASIC FURNITURE FOR THE CHAMBER

A repertoire of such furniture would include a rack, ceiling chains, and a "horse." Each of these is ideally suited to fix the submissive in one of the three basic disciplinarian postures: lying (face up or face down) in a spread-eagle position; standing with arms together or spread, and with feet either together or spread; and bent at the waist over a soft surface.

The most practical kind of rack can be constructed from a wooden frame raised on legs (to an ideal height of perhaps two and a half to three feet). Into the frame can be fitted a mattress (or not depending on the feel you want to give your submissive). This frame can be fitted with eyebolts and a chain run around the edge of the frame through these eyebolts. This creates an infinite variety of points to which the submissive can be bound. Of course, a bed or futon can also be modified as your imagination guides you and similar effects can be attained.

Chains can be dropped from the ceiling toward the middle of the room for freestanding positions, or next to the wall for more support. If these are hung in the room you normally use for some other purpose, you can always hang plants from them when they're not being used to hang a submissive! But be sure that the chains are always anchored in solid wood and able to bear significant weight—but do not try to suspend your submissive completely off the ground unless you know how to use the special equipment necessary to do this effectively and safely. Crossbars or spreader bars can also be used to ensure that the submissive will not be able to put his or her arms or legs together. These can be easily constructed out of doweling (from half an inch to one inch in diameter) with eyebolts in the ends to which the cuffs can be attached with snap hooks.

One of our favorite pieces of classic bondage furniture is the "horse." It is basically designed like a "sawhorse" with substantial padding on the top. The submissive can lie either long-wise or crosswise across the horse, be bound or not—to suffer the application of various techniques. Most classically it is used for birchings and canings. A horse can be easily moved around the house or chamber, and even be moved from location to location.

ADVANCED FURNITURE

Among the more advanced pieces of furniture are the so-called St. Andrew's Cross (an x-shaped cross), St. George's Cross (a

+-shaped cross), and the whipping post. Each of these requires special construction and is usually a permanent feature in the chamber (although clever mobile versions of each have been invented in the past).

Perhaps the greatest initial practical value of these instruments is purely aesthetic—in these arts the aesthetic is the practical. The appearance of these apparati contributes greatly to the atmospheric appeal and aura of mystery in the chamber.

The St. Andrew's Cross is useful for binding submissives in a standing position with arms and legs spread. Submissives can be comfortably bound to the St. Andrew's with either their faces or backs to the cross. The cross is often slated or tilted back to about a 45- to 70-degree angle so that the submissives can be bound up so their feet do not touch the floor.

The St. George's Cross can be free-standing or mounted on a wall of the chamber. Typically the arms of the cross are substantially higher than the head of any submissive that would be bound to it. It is a way to tie the submissive with his or her arms spread and feet together. It is ideal for whipping or any other torment. Actual "crucifixion" (that is, "fixing to a cross") in which the submissive is tied to the cross by his or her hands and feet in the position usually associated with Christ is an advanced technique, which can cause serious injury, and should not be tried except by those who have been trained.

The whipping post is a freestanding vertical post or column. It, along with the other advanced items of equipment discussed here, is also a popular feature in outdoor "torture gardens." When submissives are bound to the whipping post their hands are usually bound together stretched straight above their heads, and their feet are usually also bound together at the base of the post, although eyebolts in a platform out of which the post rises are often also used to spread their legs. These positions are ideal for whippings and lashings of all kinds.

These kinds of equipment must always be properly secured to solid anchors in walls, floors, or the ground. If not, such large objects may tip over at the worst possible times, causing a dangerous, not to mention embarrassing, situation.

Let us stress that these few pieces of equipment are only a small selection of the possible variety of devices, but they are among the most basic and pragmatic for all kinds of circumstances.

The present discussion also concentrates on what might perhaps be called a "classic" European S/M aesthetic. This by no means exhausts the possibilities for a chamber for the Working of Carnal Alchemy. Some might have a "medical aesthetic" with white tile and medical furniture and equipment, while others might appear to be an old-fashioned woodshed, a schoolroom, or some other symbolically charged atmosphere that excites the sexual feelings of the participants.

The impressive appearance of the chamber can add a great deal to the overall experience of those working within it. The chamber can become holy space, imbued with its own spirit and power. The creation of a sensory experience in the chamber is not just "smoke and mirrors," it is a real part of this type of magic. Therefore the elaborate construction of a chamber with heavy crosses, mirrors, black walls, and racks lined with fine whips, canes, and paddles is, if not necessary, certainly desirable—although all this may cause some problems if you ever have occasion to sell your house!

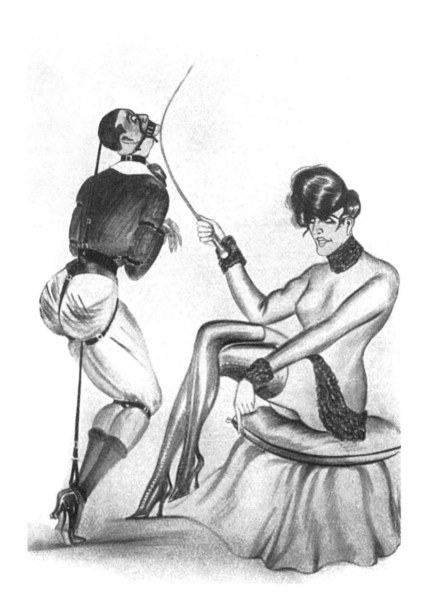

CONCLUSION

In the field of Carnal Alchemy this little volume represents only a beginning. The real mysteries can only pass by means of contact between flesh and flesh, between heart and heart, between soul and soul. Such passages have never been chronicled in a book, nor will they ever be, because they are miraculous and shrouded in eternal mystery. Almost all real work of this kind takes place between and among those who love one another and in their own secret places.

Although this book is full of hints and clues, often hiding behind what seem to be explicit instructions, no "cookbook" approach to this kind of sexuality and to this kind of spirituality is possible. The true essence of it is much too individualized for that. What works for one person or for one couple or group is sure not to work for another. This is because in essence, although Sado-Magic is keyed to experience in the objective universe, its ultimate domain is in the subjective universe beyond the constraints of this world—and ultimately in a place beyond the constraints of Heaven and Hell.

Although jokes about dominant and submissive sexuality abound on network sitcoms and feature films, this can only be taken as a sign of just how taboo this type of sexuality remains. Today many sexual variations have been accepted, if not condoned, by the political and cultural establishment. However, Sadean sexuality has enjoyed little of this acceptance or understanding. The degree to which D-S or S-M sexuality remains taboo is a barometer of its potential power.

From a woman's point of view, it seems that true liberation means the freedom of each individual woman to pursue whatever form of sexual experience that makes her happy, regardless of the standards of behavior set by any group or organization that has established itself to "look out for our best interests." There is also a definite sense that women are judged more harshly by unsympathetic men and women for being into S-M in the first place. This judgment comes from many quarters—from feminist critics to patriarchal moralists. Because it is as taboo as it is, and because it is especially so for women, the experience of S-M sexuality can be a doubly liberating adventure. But it is only liberating if it comes from your sex, heart, and true will—and is not the result of pressures from the outside.

Perhaps the "politically correct" out there will protest that what we have written here is nothing short of a sick display catering to an array of typical puerile male fantasies and that such ideas are at the bottom of all that is wrong with the world today. We do not wish to defend ourselves against such opinions because we have no interest in explaining anything to people incapable of understanding.

There are many who would be able to understand but who, nevertheless, have had their natural abilities and sensitivities warped by the forces of "civilization." It is to those we would like to address ourselves in conclusion.

The shelves of our bookstores are full of works purporting to tell couples how to "communicate" better, and how to have stronger and more intimate "relationships." Therapists and pseudotherapists prey on the fact that people cannot communicate and that their relationships are empty and without intimacy. Yet despite the flood of books and proliferation of "therapists" in the world the problems continue to grow.

For a couple to engage in a true S-M relationship, as we have discussed it here, they must communicate and there must be true intimacy in order for it to work at all. If a couple can engage in Sadean sexuality over a period of time, which fulfills both parties, it is likely that the roots of the couple's relationships are strong. But if they are weak or twisted, the intimacy necessary to the continued enjoyment of this type of sexuality will be lacking, and the activity will become impossible to sustain.

It is in this area of intimacy between individuals, between lovers, in which some of the greatest magic of Carnal Alchemy can be worked in the world today. Through this kind of magic individuals can be transformed, which, in turn, will lead to the transformation of relationships, which is a gateway to a metamorphosis of the world itself.

THE ORDER OF THE TRISKELION

The Order of the Triskelion was established for the realization of the fantasies of its members. We have a sophisticated understanding of the Sadean philosophy embedded in the myth of Roissy and the *Story of O,* and we seek to make that philosophy flesh in a safe and discreet environment.

Our main purpose is the continuing and deepening of the Sadean experiences and relationships of our members. We are interested in facilitating aesthetic experiences in the flesh and souls of those who participate with us. It can be a transforming experience. We are also concerned with the development of a social circle of those who understand this aspect of life and have the desire to share it with others. It is our intention to enhance the depth of experience of our members without exposing them to real physical or psychological dangers.

SADEANISM AND MASOCHISM

Often called by many other names—Sado-Masochism (S/M), bondage and discipline (B/D), or dominance and submission (D/S)—Sadeanism is the art and practice of deriving erotic pleasure from the infliction of bondage, discipline, humiliation, and/or pain. Masochism is the erotic enjoyment of such suffering. This is always in a mutually consensual environment. Perhaps the most elegant definition of Sadeanism—from the dominant's perspective—is "the pleasure felt from the observed modifications on the external world produced by the Will of the observer." Here, the observer is the dominant who feels the submissive struggle in bondage, sees red welts rise on the flesh, or hears those faint whimpers as the submissive is ordered to perform some humiliating task.

Probably most important to the success of our philosophy is the development and maintenance of a special link between the emotions of the submissive and those of the dominant. This sympathy—or empathy—is essential to deep-level experience of Sadeanism. Deep-level experience is the reason the Order exists.

Many in the O∴ T∴ felt that its activities cut to the very radical, root level of human life—to the psychoerotic nature of humanity and to the fundamental questions of the polarities between all extremes of human experience. Basic to this polarity are, of course, those between pleasure and pain and between the soul and the body. The Order takes this radical and pragmatic view of these models and seeks to open the pathways between these polarities in the most direct ways possible.

HISTORY OF THE ORDER

The ultimate origins of the O∴ T∴ lie shrouded in Mystery. Some say that it was founded in the late 1800s by a group of decadent French and expatriate English "Rosicrucians" in Paris who had discovered the secrets of a "carnal alchemy" and sought to preserve them in the form of a kind of sexual order. According to this version the author Pauline Réage revealed the essence of the O∴ T∴ in her book, *Story of O*. In that work there are thought to be several clues as to the reality behind the fiction. Three of the most obvious would be the references to the symbol used as the identifying mark of the slaves of Roissy: the triskelion, the name of the chateau itself; Roissy, which is said to be pun on the name of the parent order (Roissy-Croix); and the name of the central protagonist in Réage's story—"O" which is said to be a pun on the magical element eau (French for "water") being transformed in the narrative. O is transformed into the essence of wisdom (sophia) as portrayed in her final apotheosis behind the mask of an owl—a symbol for the wisdom of Athena.

But another and perhaps to some more credible version has it that the Order was founded by a group of enthusiasts for the book in the late 1960s and that it only slowly evolved from what began as a "sex-club" in Holland and Germany into a more sophisticated organization and philosophy.

Neither of these historical scenarios is easy to prove, as the O∴ T∴ is made up of fairly small groups or cells of two to six couples and the select individuals they choose to initiate. But as it exists now the Order does have a comprehensive set of teachings, practices, and ceremonies.

In the 1980s the Order was reconstituted in the United

States, and it worked magically in the underground throughout that decade to bring the S/M philosophy to wider acceptance in the general public. Its main manifesto, Carnal Alchemy, began to circulate privately in manuscript form in the early 1990s and was originally published in 1994. By the mid-1990s the Order again went underground given the newly widespread popularity of S/M.

THE PHILOSOPHY OF "O"

In the classic novel by Pauline Réage, *Story of O,* there lies concealed a great philosophical and virtually mystical message. It is a message of personal transformation and change of the path of the human soul on the road to empowerment and even transcendence.

The philosophy of O is a sensual/aesthetic one—based on strong sensual contrasts—and its purpose is the transformation of the personality through psychosensual experience. For O the experience of great dualities—pain/pleasure, bondage/liberation, dominance/submission, pride/humiliation leads to this ecstatic change.

O allows herself to be molded by artists of the craft of sexual domination, but she never loses the reality of the inner control of herself, nor do her Masters desire her to do so—her submission is always and continuously a conscious act of her own will. This is fundamental to the eternal path of O.

A keystone of the philosophy of O is her relationship to the other human beings around her. O's philosophy is a decidedly sociosexual one, although this is not the case in all Sadean myths. She allows herself to be "given," and since this is essentially an act of her own will, she succeeds in further objectifying her ego in yet another step toward self-realization.

THE PHILOSOPHY OF THE ORDER

The inner essence of the O∴ T∴ can be summed up in the formula of "carnal alchemy." This is a psychoerotic process by which 1) the contents of the imagination are stimulated, 2) transformed into volition, and then 3) made flesh—or actual carnal experience. This is the essence of the so-called Triskelion Process, which many of the Masters of the Order undertake with their Slaves.

Through this threefold process the inner alchemy, which turns pain into pleasure, bondage into liberation, and humiliation into pride, is stimulated. These pathways in the body/mind are so deeply rooted that it is found that once these pathways are opened in this context they begin to open in other areas of life as well.

The Order advocates a whole set of aesthetics and a way of behavioralizing a complete Sadean relationship. The basic unit of working within the Order is the couple in some kind of committed relationship. The dominant and the submissive subtly work together to arrive at a whole range of things (techniques, scenarios, personas, etc.) that go into creating an alternate universe that belongs to the Dominant and Submissive in partnership. It is the responsibility of the Master or Mistress to discover what their Slaves desire, fantasize about, and want (and fear) to be fulfilled in their experiences in the flesh. In this activity the Master can have no initial set of established techniques or anything else. The whole relationship develops as a complex dance between the two persons involved. It is the task of the Master to see that the Slaves are fulfilled and that their deepest fantasies are realized. This is the path of a true "dialog" between not only the essences of the Master and Slave, but on another level between the flesh and the spirit of the persons involved. This process is essential to the opening of the pathways between the polarities: between the world of dream and imagination and that of the reality of the flesh.

STRUCTURE OF THE ORDER

The O∴ T∴ was made up of independent cells chartered by the central lodge. These cells exercised the philosophy of the Order independently at their own discretion. The central lodge bore no responsibility for how the various cells were run, and they may vary in practices and rituals one from the other.

ENTRY INTO THE ORDER

For details on the possibilities of entry into the Order, or on receiving a Charter for the foundation of a cell of the Order, please write to the publisher of this book, or use the e-mail address runa@texas.net.

RESOURCES

Of course there are dozens of organizations and providers of services and products and publications dedicated to the S-M lifestyle. What we offer here is just a sampling of some of the better-known and most permanent and reliable representatives in these fields. The authors welcome feedback on these and correspondence concerning other organizations and service providers.

Order of the Triskelion
P.O. Box 557
Smithville, Texas 78957

Headed by Stephen and Crystal Dawn Flowers, this was the only organization in the world dedicated to the pursuit of Carnal Alchemy.

The Eulenspiegel Society
P.O. Box 2783
Grand Central Station
New York, NY 10163
E-mail: TES@tes.org

This is one of the oldest continuously active organizations openly educating the public in the field of S-M in the United States. It meets in New York City.

The National Leather Association (NLA) and **People Exchanging Power (PEP)** have local organizations in various places around the USA.

Locating other organizations and networks dedicated to the pursuit of S-M sexuality is best pursued via the Internet. A search of "bdsm organizations" will result in over a hundred organizations all over the country and around the world.

NOTES

PREFACE TO THE FIRST EDITION

1. Frater U/D/, *Secrets of the German Sex Magician,* 193.

CHAPTER 1. SEXUAL MAGIC AND CARNAL ALCHEMY

1. Crowley, *The Magical Record of the Beast 666,* 131.
2. King, *Sexuality, Magic and Perversion,* 36.

CHAPTER 2. SADO-MAGIC IN HISTORY

1. De Sade, *Justine, Philosophy of the Bedroom, and Other Writings,* discussed by Gorer in *The Life and Times of the Marquis de Sade,* 180.
2. Sacher-Masoch, cited in Deleuze, *Coldness and Cruelty,* 275.
3. Deleuze, *Coldness and Cruelty,* 94.
4. Gardner, "Book of Shadows" in *Crafting the Art of Magic.*
5. Kelly, *Crafting the Art of Magic,* 81.
6. LaVey, cited in Barton, *The Secret Life of a Satanist,* 182.
7. Gorer, *The Life and Times of the Marquis de Sade,* 187.

CHAPTER 7. WORKING TECHNIQUES

1. Frater U/D/, *Secrets of the German Sex Magician,* 194.

GLOSSARY

alchemy: A worldwide spiritual phenomenon best known as a technology for transformation—of base things into noble things (e.g., lead into gold), or mortal things into immortal ones. It is characterized by complex processes, which involve the breakdown of substances into their component elements to create perfect substances. The word comes from the Arabic phrase meaning "the art of Egypt (Khemet)," eventually simplified to "chemistry."

Carnal Alchemy: The use of Sadean methods to effect the purposes of Alchemy. Used for self-transformational purposes and distinguished from Sado-Magic and Sado-Shamanism in that it is not generally applied to specific situations at all but rather is used for initiatory purposes.

dominant: A generic term for a participant in D/S or S/M sexual activity who has consensually agreed to be an active facilitator of Sadean methods as applied to a submissive. Some people feel they are dominant by sexual nature, others may be equally dominant and submissive. Commonly also called a "Top."

initiation: A gradual, rationally designed evolution of essence of a person from one state of being to another.

macrocosm: Greek for "big world." This is the objective universe and the whole of the order of Nature.

magic: The willed use of symbolic methods to cause or present changes in the universe by means of symbolic acts of communication with paranormal factors. These factors could be inside or outside the subjective universe of the operator. Magic is a way to cause things to happen that would not happen naturally or ordinarily.

Masochism: Originally coined after the name of the Austrian writer Leopold von Sacher-Masoch, who was a literary pioneer in the area of depictions of consensual D/S sexuality. As we use it, the term *Masochism* has little to do with the psychopathological description.

microcosm: Greek for "little world." This is the subjective universe and the body of the individual human being.

objective universe: This is the "outer world" shared by all individuals. The part of existence that can be perceived by the five senses, it is the mechanical/organic order characterized by its regularity and predictability, by the presence of the laws of nature.

operative: A more technically descriptive term for what is usually called "magical." Something is operative if it acts as a tool or means by which a change or alteration is effected.

Sadeanism: A generic, yet poetic, term for D/S sexuality. Not to be confused with the psychopathological term "Sadism," with which it has little to nothing in common.

Sado-Magic: The use of Sadean methods to effect the purposes of Magic. Differentiated from Sado-Shamanism in that Sado-Magic is usually applied to cause some specific ultimate result in the objective universe.

Sado-Shamanism: The use of Sadean methods to effect the purposes of Shamanism. Differentiated from Sado-Magic in that Sado-Shamanism is usually applied to correct some specific problem or effect some specific result in the subjective universe(s) of the participants.

sexual magic: Any use of sexuality, sexual symbolism, or the energy of the human orgasm to effect the aims of magic.

shamanism: This is a much misunderstood and misused word of late. It is primarily a "technique of ecstasy" in which usually physical methods are used to trigger ecstatic states and/or trance-like states in which deep realms of one's own, or other subjective universes, become consciously known.

subjective universe: This is the "inner world" of the individual, the "world" of any thinking entity within the universe. There are as many subjective universes as there are thinking beings.

submissive: This is a generic term for a participant in D/S or S/M sexual activity who has consensually agreed to be a recipient of Sadean methods as applied by a dominant. Some people feel they are submissive by sexual nature; others may be equally submissive and dominant. Commonly also called a "Bottom."

tantrism: A philosophical and religious tradition found in both Hinduism and Buddhism. It is characterized by taboo-breaking practices, the worship of the Goddess (a contra-sexual deity), and by sexual symbolism.

Universe: The totality of existence, known and unknown.

AN ANNOTATED
SADEAN
BIBLIOGRAPHY

FICTIONAL WORKS

Often the best clues to the practice of Carnal Alchemy are not to be found in "how-to" books, or in "cookbook" approaches to magic—but rather between the lines in the great works of fiction written from the heart of darkness in the center of each of the authors of literary works such as those that we present here.

Anonymous. *Beatrice.* New York: Grove Press, 1982.
> Extremely well-written novel of sexual enslavement in the English countryside—with some special emphasis on equestrian training.

Anonymous. *The Days at Florville.* New York: Grove Press, 1983.
> This book is continued in *The Gardens of the Night* and *Beatrice* and must count as the great "Victorian" classics of D/S. It is perhaps in this work and the others that the "O-Mythos" was first engendered. It traces the sexual enslavement of Lesley

within a secret brotherhood, the exact limits of which remain unknown.

Anonymous. *The Gardens of the Night.* New York: Grove Press, 1985.

> Apparently written by the same author who wrote *Days at Florville,* of which it is the continuation. This work takes us deeper into the underground international network—and takes Lesley deeper into the realms of voluptuous slavery. It features some severe forms of discipline and ingenious and imaginative forms of punishment.

Anonymous. *Tomboy: Revelations of a Girls' Reformatory.* New York: Grove Press, 1986.

> Erotic glimpse into the deliciously cruel culture of English girls' reformatories of the Victorian Age. This book features descriptions of severe canings and birchings.

Berg, Jean de. *The Image.* Translated by Patsy Southgate. New York: Grove Press, 1966.

> Originally published in France in 1956. This work appeared just two years after *Story of O* and was graced with a preface by Pauline Réage herself. It is the only work to have come close to matching the modern mythic appeal of *Story of O.* This book was the basis of a film released under both the titles, *The Image* and *The Punishment of Anne.*

Berg, Jeanne de. *Women's Rites.* Translated by Anselm Hollo. New York: Grove Press, 1987.

> Translated from a 1985 French collection, *Ceremonies de femmes,* this book is supposed to be by the wife of the author of *The Image.* It portrays an elegant world of European D/S sexuality

from a female dominant perspective and gives a wonderful glimpse into the mind of the sexually dominant personality.

Califia, Pat. *Macho Sluts*. Boston: Alyson Press, 1988.

This collection of short stories is remarkable for the deep-level insight it gives into the psychology of the dominant persona. The writing talent necessary to do this is extraordinary. From this literary perspective it is perhaps the best work of S/M fiction since *Story of O*. Its viewpoint is pansexual, which makes the writing achievement even more impressive.

Coover, Robert. *Spanking the Maid*. New York: Grove Press, 1988.

This is a highly erotic postmodern novel in which the metaphor of corporal punishment is used to reveal a hidden magical world beyond the facade of appearances.

McNeill, Elizabeth. *Nine and A Half Weeks*. New York: E. P. Dutton, 1978.

Supposedly a true story. If true, it would seem that the man in the story was a half-trained Chateau-valet. Some of the techniques used by him are valid, but he did not know how to apply them gracefully—and he paid the price! Despite this his "Elizabeth" has provided us with a highly erotic account of her experiences. The book was the basis of a film, but not one that does the book any justice.

Rampling, Anne. (= Anne Rice). *Exit to Eden*. New York: Arbor House, 1985.

As a philosophical statement and as a manual of practical dream-weaving, this work is the most compelling D/S work since *Story of O*. It is primarily from the female dominant, male submissive perspective, which makes it doubly important, as little good literature exists from this angle. "The Club" as described in the book is based on the idea of Roissy.

Réage, Pauline. *Story of O.* Translated by Sabine d'Estree. New York: Grove Press, 1965.

Originally published in France in 1954, this is the great modern classic against which all others are measured. The book was the basis of a faithful film adaptation released under the title *The Story of O.*

Roquelaure, A. N. (= Anne Rice). *Beauty's Punishment.* New York: E. P. Dutton, 1984.

A continuation of the Beauty series, and perhaps the best of the trilogy.

Roquelaure, A. N. (= Anne Rice). *Beauty's Release.* New York: E. P. Dutton, 1985.

A continuation of the Beauty trilogy, and certainly its most exotic.

Roquelaure, A. N. (= Anne Rice). *The Claiming of Sleeping Beauty.* New York: E. P. Dutton, 1983.

This, along with its two sequels, forms the basis of an alternate mythos to the "O-Mythos" with which it shares many character-istics. It creates a fairy-tale universe—a Sado-Masochistic utopia that all should visit.

Sacher-Masoch, Leopold von. *Venus in Furs.* Translated by Jean McNeil. In *Masochism.* New York: Zone Books, 1989.

A volume in Masoch's projected Heritage of Cain series, it is a classic study of male Masochism that illustrates much of the modern and postmodern mythology of S/M.

NONFICTION WORKS

Although there are many books on the subject of Sado-Masochism, most published before 1990 were written from a purely psychopathological viewpoint—which means that they were virtually worthless to the Sado-Magician. There are some exceptions. In the early 1990s there was a flood of "how-to" books on S-M, not all of uniform quality. Each of the books presented in this category is unique and special in some respect, and assimilation of the contents of these works will make anyone a better practitioner of Carnal Alchemy.

Anthony, Edward. *Thy Rod and Staff.* London: Abacus, 1996.
>   A wide-ranging study of the flagellant experience notable for its extensive discussions of the ritual aspects of the "English vice" and the importance of archetypal roles assumed by the participants.

Baldwin, Guy. *Ties That Bind: The SM/Leather/Fetish Erotic Style.* Los Angeles: Daedalus, 1993.
>   Although this is an anthology of articles from gay male magazines, the psychospiritual dimensions he discusses are universal human ones. The issues range from those more properly defined as mental or emotional health to the attainment of a transformational psychomystical state of being.

Califia, Pat, ed. *The Lesbian S/M Safety Manual.* Boston: Lace/Alyson, 1988.
>   Informative collection of essays on all aspects of safety in S/M activity. Here safety includes emotional as well as physical considerations.

Califia, Pat. *Sensuous Magic: A Guide for Adventurous Couples*. New York: Richard Kasak, 1993.

> Although this book is not about magic in the definition we use, its contents can be considered magical in themselves in that they can open doorways to experience among people who have not considered the spiritual dimension of S-M.

Cowan, Lyn. *Masochism: A Jungian View*. Dallas, Tex.: Spring Publications, 1982.

> This book offers valuable insight into the positive psychological effects and functions of Masochism. It should be read by all healthy and self-aware and self-affirming submissives—and by those who would dominate them.

Deforges, Regine. *Confessions of O: Conversations with Pauline Réage*. Translated by Sabine d'Estree. New York: Viking Press, 1979.

> This work, which is written in the style of an interview with "Pauline Réage," offers otherwise impossible to obtain insight into the mind that created the "O-Mythos." We are afforded a glimpse into the origins of it—in Anglophilism, for example.

Deleuze, Gilles. *Coldness and Cruelty*. Translated by Jean McNeil. In *Masochism*. New York: Zone Books, 1989.

> An insightful study of the life, work, and philosophy of Leopold von Sacher-Masoch and the relationship of that philosophy to that of Sade.

Gorer, Geoffrey. *The Life and Ideas of the Marquis de Sade*. 2nd ed. London: Owen, 1953

> Gorer's study of Sade is the most insightful and philosophically sophisticated yet produced. A basic understanding of Sade's thought is intellectually beneficial to the Sado-Magician and

can give some understanding of the physical aspects of Carnal Alchemy, although ultimately Sade's philosophy is too short-sighted to serve as a framework for a total theory of how pleasure and pain can be used for self-transformation.

Greene, Gerald and Caroline. *S-M: The Last Taboo*. New York: Grove Press, 1974.

This is perhaps the best general nonfiction book ever published on the subject of algolagnia. It is written from the viewpoint of those who actually practice the arts, in an open healthy way. It is philosophically sound and includes a variety of some of the best D/S erotic fiction as appendices.

Jacques, Trevor. *On the Safe Edge: A Manual for SM Play*. Toronto: WholeSM, 1993.

This might best be defined as an extensive SM safety manual—its topics range from technical safety during a scene to aspects of mental and physical health.

Midori. *The Seductive Art of Japanese Rope Bondage*. Emeryville, Calif.: Greenery Press, 2001.

A good and basic how-to manual on the techniques of Japanese rope bondage.

Miller, Philip, and Molly Devon. *Screw the Roses, Send Me the Thorns: The Romance and Sexual Sorcery of Sadomasochism*. Fairfield, Conn.: Mystic Rose Books, 1995.

Here is a highly informative and heavily illustrated guide to the general principles of S-M sexuality. Recommended for beginners in S-M who cannot find a group to work with. Like other books, which hint at "magic" in their titles, this one has nothing to do with magic, as we, or other practicing magicians, would define it. However, the repeated use of the word "magic" in connection with conventional S-M does show the degree to which it is widely held that there is something intrinsically *mysterious* about S-M in general.

Scott, Gini G. *Erotic Power: An Exploration of Dominance and Submission*. Seacaucus, N.J.: Citadel, 1983.

Scott's book was published earlier under the title *Dominant Women, Submissive Men*, which is really more descriptive of the material in the book. It is a sympathetic study of the D/S scene written from a sociological perspective. It contains some insights into the "religious" and ritual elements of the culture but really does not go beyond the surface, as the author is a sociologist, not a magician.

Wiseman, Jay. *SM 101: A Realistic Introduction*. Berkeley, Calif.: Author, 1992.

This is a classic introduction to safe, sane, and consensual S-M, with many ideas on how to find and negotiate with potential partners.

BIBLIOGRAPHY OF GENERAL TITLES AND SEX-MAGICAL TEXTS

Andreae, Johann Valentin. *The Chymical Wedding of Christian Rosencreutz.* Strasbourg, Ger.: N.p., 1616.

Barton, Blanche. *The Secret Life of a Satanist. The Authorized Biography of Anton Szandor LaVey.* Los Angeles: Feral House, 1990.

Bataille, Georges. *Erotism: Death and Sensuality.* Translated by M. Dalwood. San Francisco: City Lights, 1986.

Baudelaire, Charles. *Les Fleurs du Mal.* Translated by R. Howard. Boston: David R. Godine, 1982.

Bornoff, Nicholas. *Pink Samurai: Love, Marriage & Sex in Compemporary Japan.* New York: Pocket, 1991.

Burkert, Walter. *Ancient Mystery Cults.* Cambridge, Mass.: Harvard University Press, 1987.

Crowley, Aleister. *The Magical Record of the Beast 666.* London: Duckworth, 1972.

Culling, Louis. *A Manual of Sex Magic.* St. Paul, Minn.: Llewellyn, 1971.

Eliade, Mircea. *Shamanism: Archaic Techniques of Ecstasy.* Translated by W. Trask. Princeton: Princeton University Press, 1964.

Evola, Julius. *The Metaphysics of Sex.* New York: Inner Traditions, 1983.

Flowers, Stephen E. *The Fraternitas Saturni.* 3rd ed. Smithville, Tex.: Rûna-Raven, 2006.

———. *Lords of the Left-Hand Path.* Rochester, Vt.: Inner Traditions, 2012.

Frater U\D\. *Secrets of the German Sex Magicians.* Translated by Ingrid Fischer. St. Paul, Minn.: Llewellyn, 1991.

Gennep, Arnold van. *Rites of Passage.* Translated by M. Vizedom and G. Caffee. Chicago: University of Chicago Press, 1960.

Gorer, Geoffrey. *The Life and Ideas of the Marquis de Sade.* 2nd ed. London: Peter Owen, 1953,

Kelly, Aidan. *Crafting the Art of Magic.* St. Paul, Minn.: Llewellyn, 1991.

King, Francis. *Sexuality, Magic and Perversion.* London: Neville Spearman, 1971.

———. *The Secret Rituals of the O.T.O.* New York: Weiser, 1973.

———. *Tantra for Westerners.* New York: Destiny, 1986.

Lucretius. *On the Nature of the Universe.* Translated by R. Latham. Harmondsworth, U.K.: Penguin, 1951.

Meyer, Gerd. "Verfehmter Nächte blasser Sohn: Ein erster Blick auf Ernst Schertel." In *Phantom Schmerz.* Edited by Michael Farin. Munich: Belleville, 2003.

Mookojee, Ajit, and Madhu Khana. *The Tantric Way.* Boston: New York Graphic Society, 1977.

Naglowska, Maria de. *Advanced Sex Magic: The Hanging Mystery Initiation.* Translated by Donald Traxler. Rochester, Vt.: Inner Traditions, 2011.

North, Robert. *The New Flesh Palladium: Magia Sexualis.* Smithville, Tex.: Rûna-Raven Press, 1995.

———. *The Grimoire of Maria de Naglowska.* Miami: New Flesh Palladium, 2009.

Randolph, Paschal Beverly. *Sexual Magic.* Translated by Robert North. New York: Magickal Childe, 1988.

Sade, Marquis de. *The Marquis de Sade: The Complete Justine, Philosophy in the Bedroom, and Other Writings.* Translated by R. Seaver and A. Wainhouse. New York: Grove, 1966.

———. *The 120 Days of Sodom and Other Writings.* Translated by R. Seaver and A. Wainhouse. New York: Grove, 1966.

———. *Juliette.* Translated by R. Seaver and A. Wainhouse. New York: Grove, 1968.

Seabrook, William. *Witchcraft: Its Power in the World Today.* New York: Harcourt, Brace, 1940.

Sellon, Edward. *Annotations upon the Sacred Writing of the Hindus.* London: New Edition of London, 1865.

Steddinger, Inga. *Wiccan Sex-Magic.* Smithville, Tex.: Rûna-Raven, 1999.

Toepfer, Karl. *Empire of Ecstasy: Nudity and Movement in German Body-Culture 1910-1935.* Berkeley: University of California Press, 1997.

Walker, Benjamin. *Tantrism.* Wellingborough, U.K.: Aquarian Press, 1982.

INDEX